C000112850

MURIEL'S CHILDREN

Muriel's Children

MARY CUNDY

eagle

Guildford, Surrey

British Library Cataloguing in Publication Data. A catalogue
record for this book is available from the British Library.

Published by Eagle, an imprint of Inter Publishing Service
(IPS) Ltd, 6-7 Leapale Road, Guildford, Surrey GU1 4JX.

Typeset by Eagle Publishing
Printed by Cox & Wyman
ISBN No: 0 86347 293 1

CONTENTS

MURIEL

A life dedicated to God and abandoned babies
with the Nurseries Fellowship, Gorakhpur, India

PREFACE

I first met Muriel Ainger in the 1940s when she came as a missionary speaker to a Girl Crusaders' Union camp. I was a Junior Officer and Muriel's lifelong friend, Norah Lloyd, was the Commandant. Muriel had then been about twenty years caring for destitute and orphan children in a home founded by Miss M. Warburton Booth in Gorakhpur, India, called the Nurseries Fellowship. She had dedicated her life to this 'family'.

She made a never-to-be-forgotten impression on me, not because of the work she was doing, sacrificial as it appeared, but for some indefinable integrity of character that shone out from her. I realised at that early stage in my Christian life that she knew Jesus Christ in a way I didn't.

I had at that time no thought of going overseas to work. But in 1957 God called me to the once closed land of Nepal, just over the border from Gorakhpur.

So our paths crossed again, when I stopped at the Nurseries on my way into Nepal. I had another link with the Nurseries, as Miss Ivy Hill (always known as 'Matie') had been the Matron of the Maternity Home in Clapham and my mother's midwife when I was born. She had been, as she described it, 'gloriously converted' at the age of fifty and had subsequently gone out to join the Gorakhpur family.

Since Gorakhpur was the railhead into Nepal, and the last big town before crossing the border, I visited and stayed frequently at the Nurseries, forging links of friendship with Muriel.

Muriel was to stay sixty years in Gorakhpur, only coming home at the age of eighty-four in 1988 to live in a bungalow she was left in the beautiful village of Blakeney on the north Norfolk coast.

We were to be near each other, too, at the end of her life, as for her last few years she came to live in Tunbridge Wells, and I retired from Nepal to a cottage in the village of Matfield. The cottage, incidentally, had been left to me by Miss Irene Cleeve, who had been General Secretary of the Girl Crusaders' Union, the organisation through which Muriel and I had originally met!

However, in spite of all those links and friendship with Muriel, in no way would I have thought of writing a book about her. So, when after she died in 1995 I sensed God saying to me 'You are to write a book about Muriel', it seemed so ridiculous that I pushed the thought aside and did not mention it to anyone. However, as it persisted I said to God, 'Well if someone asks me to do it, I'll consider it'! I could not think of anyone who was the least likely to approach me on the subject!

Some time later, as I was helping two people down the aisle coming out of Muriel's Thanksgiving Service, someone tapped me on the shoulder and said, 'Sitting in church, Mary, I sensed God was saying the next assignment for you is to write a book about Muriel'. I turned and gaped at her!

So, for better or worse, here it is.

In the back of a book by George Appleton, I found the following Writer's Prayer by Robert Herrick (1591–1674):

For every sentence, clause and word,
that's not inlaid with thee, my Lord,
Forgive me, God, and blot each line
out of my book, that is not thine.
But if, 'mongst all, thou find'st here one
worthy thy benediction,
That one of all the rest shall be
the glory of my work and me.

1

'MAKE THE OMNIPOTENCE OF GOD THE MEASURE OF YOUR EXPECTATION'

These words, 'Make the omnipotence of God the measure of your expectation', were on a wooden plaque that Muriel Ainger had hanging behind her bed at Gorakhpur Nurseries, and it had such significance in her life that she brought it home with her, and I now have it.

Muriel was with the Gorakhpur Nurseries Fellowship in the north of India for sixty years. Sixty years – that's a long time to spend in one place. What are the Nurseries? A place where they grow vegetables? Well, they do grow vegetables, but it is to help feed the large family of orphaned and abandoned children who are given a home there; hundreds of them over the years.

How did it begin?

In 1907, a deaconess named Mary Warburton Booth, working in the East End of London, went to a meeting at the Mildmay Conference Hall in Newington Green. The speaker was a missionary from India. A missionary is very rarely, initially, an interest-arousing speaker. A traveller, a pioneer, an adventurer, he or she may be, but call him or her a missionary and you have lost half your potential audience before you start. So it was that day with Miss Warburton Booth. She was tired and absorbed with the problems she had left and although she had come to the meeting, she was not at all inclined to listen.

However as soon as the speaker started, she was grabbed, riveted and moved by what she heard. The speaker told of going to a city in India given over to idolatry. She described graphically the needs and despair of the people as they worshipped the dead idols. Then she told how the Living Christ had come with his power and light into the darkness and how lives and the place itself had been changed.

In spite of herself Mary Warburton Booth was moved. She said, 'I longed to be there, but I never thought of going.'

It was a week of meetings and she went each day, inspired to be in the large meetings. She wrote of the unforgettable experience it was to stand with the vast congregation singing 'Jesus stand among us in thy risen power'. As she did, she said she was telling the Lord that she would do anything, go anywhere, for him.

She recalled that as she was telling him, 'Lord you are so wonderful to me, I will go anywhere for you', in the silence of her heart she heard a voice say softly 'Will you go to India?' She was so sure of the voice and so startled, she turned round to see who had spoken, but there was no one behind her. She was sitting in the back seat and trembling so much that the deaconess beside her put her hand on hers and asked if she was ill.

She steadied herself to listen to the preacher. He was reading the sixth chapter of Isaiah: 'Whom shall I send? Who will go for us?'. There was a long pause and silence as if the reader searched for someone.

'The silence was intense and all my being,' she wrote, 'hearkened for the answer. He read, "Then said I, here am I, send me." '

That was all, but Mary was lifted right out of the conference centre 'into the presence of God and the recognition of an open door to be entered. I was called, the voice was so insistent. I'd never thought of being a missionary, that was for others, yet here I was, face to face with a call.'

She went back to her deaconess work and told her colleagues. They were sure she was mistaken, she was being so blessed in the work she was doing with them.

To obey God's call is never an easy matter and Mary found that this was so for her. She had to face a lot of opposition.

She applied to the then Zenana Bible and Medical Mission (now Interserve). It was, she wrote, a long testing period, so much so that she began to wonder if she should go.

Then, reading her Bible one day, she was riveted by the words, 'If you refuse to go forth'. So she braced herself and even more definitely than before set her face towards India.

In 1908 she was sent out to Gorakhpur, Uttar Pradesh (UP), North India, a town on the border of Nepal, to a work ZBMM had there in the Zenanas, as the women's quarters were then known.

Her first term was for five-and-a-half years. She worked hard learning the language, taking Bible classes, visiting people, attending prayer meetings and teaching in the Mission School, but at the end of it, she was discouraged and disappointed. There seemed to be so very little real result for all her labours. True there were several in the Zenanas who had believed in Jesus but otherwise she felt – nothing.

Her heart had, however, been moved by the arrival of a small abandoned baby three years before. There were no facilities to keep the child on the compound where they lived, so she had taken her to friends in the Salvation Army who looked after her. Mary felt, however, very responsible for her and saw her often. This was the only bit of Gorakhpur she was sorry to leave. When she said goodbye to the ladies in the Zenanas they said 'Come back soon', but she hoped that God had something better for her and it was wrapped in a special wish that she might not have to return to Gorakhpur.

It was the spring of 1914 when she returned home. She said she felt very much as the disciples did when they had caught nothing, having fished all night.

In the summer she went to the Keswick Convention. She felt no uplift at being there. She prayed and talked with people, making no secret of not wanting to go back to Gorakhpur.

Then one evening, Rev Stuart Holden spoke about the three men who were standing before the king. 'We know our God, whom we serve, is able to deliver us, but if not . . . we shall obey him just the same . . . we will not serve other gods' (Daniel 3:16–18). He went on to say, 'You came to Keswick disappointed because of the way you have trusted the Lord to do some great things and there is a blank – you have prayed for a revival and nothing has happened – and you are thinking the God whom we serve is able – but, but, but if not . . . what is your answer?'

Mary wrote:

As I sat there, one in a congregation of 3,000 people, I knew God was speaking to me. My years in Gorakhpur were like a moving picture before me, scene after scene passed by. I did not want to go back there. I wanted to try another place where, perhaps, I would be more successful. Mr. Stuart Holden was speaking, 'Will you go back to your old life where you have prayed for revival? Our God whom we serve is able – but if not?' The silence was intense. He waited as a man who knows how to wait with a message straight from God. 'But if not?' he repeated.

I listened. I knew God was speaking to me saying,

'Are you willing to go back to Gorakhpur, even if I do not give you a revival?' In the hush of the gathering darkness I said, 'Lord I am willing for anything, revival or no revival.' I would trust him and return to Gorakhpur.

The Lord took Mary at her word and, after eight months at home, she returned to Gorakhpur that same year. She hoped to find it different, but she said that even the pieces of brick lying in the courtyards through which she passed on her way to church on Sunday seemed to lie in exactly the same place as they had been when she left.

She went to the Zenanas and the people listened in the same uninterested fashion – just glad to see anyone who would break their monotonous lives. Mary had a message and wanted it to be received with joy, but it was not.

The school flourished and they worked harder than ever, but Mary still felt completely unsatisfied.

Then her senior missionary went home on leave and she was left in charge.

They had money sent from England each month by ZBMM to pay the teachers and the Bible women and to keep the work going. There was nothing to help any expansion of the work, only just enough to pay their way.

What was the way forward? What was the Lord saying to them at this point?

Mary Warburton Booth felt she should pray more about it. But the hindrances to prayer in India are legion. The climate is exhausting, the insect life is so prolific that you are reminded always that you have a body, and mosquitoes love you and insects visit you – their hunger is never satisfied. In the hot, humid climate the mosquitoes revel and they hinder concentrated prayer. For instance, she wrote, 'You kneel to pray and down comes a mosquito and gives you a nip in passing. In less than a second it is over but an irritation remains that takes your attention. You realise very vividly you are still in the flesh. Satan doesn't want us to persist in prayer and he has many devices, tiredness, mosquitoes, interruptions, laziness, climate etc. etc. to hinder us.' She prayed on however, compelled to be very definite by the dwindling finances coming to them.

There were twelve teachers and Bible women. They had worked in the Mission for years and although they did their work, sang, preached and talked they had almost got to the point of not seeing any results. There was no one leaving all and coming out for the Lord, which was what Mary Warburton Booth was longing and believing for.

She was sure that God had not brought her to India just to influence people. A farmer does not go into his field to influence it, he expects to reap crops for the seed he has sown. So it should be with the sowing of spiritual seed – we should see results. She gathered the Bible women and teachers together and prayed with them for light and understanding. They were led to open their Bibles at Malachi chapter three.

Mary Warburton Booth had just had a letter from the Zenana Mission to say that, due to lack of funds, some of the work was to be closed and expenses cut down.

With this letter in her hand Miss Warburton Booth read Malachi 3:10 to them: ' "Bring all the tithes into the storehouse and prove me now," says the Lord of Hosts, "if I will not open you the windows of heaven and pour you out a blessing there shall not be room enough to receive it." '

'Prove me now,' they read, 'bring all the tithes.' Over and over again they read the words. What are tithes they thought. Must we give tithes? If so, how much? In the Bible it said that God's people in olden times gave a tenth of all they had. Could we, they thought, give a tenth of all we have every month. If it was only ten rupees, it meant one out of the ten and there would be only nine left.

However it seemed to be God's voice to them and they promised to obey.

It was a great joy to Mary Warburton Booth when, on the first of the month the Bible women and teachers received their meagre pay, there was a readiness, and even eagerness, to pay their tithes. They gave the money away to a charity.

It was as if a burden had been lifted and a gate opened that had been fast closed, and 'expectancy', she wrote, 'took hold of me'. The message of the weekly Bible Class was, 'Ask of me and I will give you the heathen for your inheritance'.

Then, in an amazing way, women in need and especially children came – one she described as being snatched from the brink of hell.

They had a further letter saying they must entrench more, but God seemed to be sending them more children to care for. His message to them seemed to be 'not less but more, just follow me'. Then someone gave them £1,000 (a lot of money in those days) to build a bungalow needed for housing. Another letter at that time which warmed their hearts was from a Scots lass whose father had been stationed in Gorakhpur and the little girl had come to know Jesus while with them. She wrote, 'I am sending a postal order for five shillings from my pocket money and I am praying it will help some other girl to come to know Jesus.'

It was their first gift for the children and it paid for the milk a sickly child needed. They took it as an earnest of what God was going to do. Only five shillings from a little girl but it gave them a certainty that the Bank of England could never give – that if they were obedient to God and took in all whom he sent them, he would supply all their needs.

So the work that is known as the Gorakhpur Nurseries was born.

2

TO YOU FROM ME

The Gorakhpur Nurseries still receive babies and small children who have been rescued. Miss Warburton Booth wrote about one of the first in *Take This Child*. One Sunday evening, just after coming in from church, she saw a little girl of about seven standing on the verandah. When Mary Warburton Booth went to her, the little girl said, 'I have run away and come to you. You won't send me away will you?'

Miss Warburton Booth took her in her arms and into her room and bit by bit the little girl told her why she had run away and come to her. Miss Warburton Booth could scarcely believe her ears, but a Voice seemed to say to her, 'These things happen all around you, she is only one of thousands, help her, let her tell it all out.' So she did.

The next day she had to take her to the local Collector. At that time India was part of the British Empire, known as the British Raj or rule. They appointed men to be responsible for an area who were known as Collectors. He heard her story and, as he was just leaving for camp, he asked Mary Warburton Booth to keep her and said he would be in touch. In the waiting time, the little girl would often put her hand in Miss Warburton Booth's and say, 'You will let me stay with you always won't you?'

She had run away from being trained for an immoral life. She could sing, she was learning to dance. Her little body bore burn marks where the man, who called himself her father, had held matches to her to bring her to submission. He had also tied her with cords.

She had seen the Nurseries folk from a distance when they had gone out to the villages and something – Someone – had caused her to know that they could be trusted and so she came, drawn by an unseen hand, through hearing a hymn, a smile or who knows what, but she came.

As she told her story, they wondered how she could have borne it all and how she had got away. It felt in a special way that God had brought her to them.

Then after she had been with them ten days, the man from whom she had fled, arrived. He broke into a tirade of abuse at Miss Warburton Booth. 'You have bewitched her,' he said. 'You have caused a spell to spin over her. She is my valuable property. You cannot have her.'

Others joined him and called for the child to come. Miss Warburton Booth called her forward and told the man to ask her to return with him, but she just clung to Miss Warburton Booth. In the end he went off, swearing he would bring an order against her for bewitching the child. Next day a very important looking police official, bedecked in gold braid, arrived. He asked about the little girl who had been bewitched and enticed away from her father. He asked to see her and was amazed when she came forward unafraid. He said she would have to return to her father, to which she replied that the man was not her father. This seemed to surprise the official and even more so when she said he had bought her from her mother for twenty annas (about 20p).

She then told how, after her father died, her mother went on a pilgrimage to Bernares, Ajudiya, Gaya and other places. The priests had told her she would get peace if she gave up her daughter. She refused, but when she had given all her jewellery to the priests and had nothing left, she was again told that she would have peace if she gave her daughter up to the gods. So, in the end, tired and weary, she sold her daughter for twenty annas; and died two days later.

The gold-braided official wrote it all down and took it to his superior officer. Two days later the 'head of affairs' arrived. He was known as a man without a heart so they did not expect help from him. The little girl was very calm as she repeated her story. The man was not her father – he had bought her for twenty annas from her mother. There followed a court case, when the man who claimed to be her father came up with all manner of lies, and brought witnesses to prove them, including someone who said that he knew the man was the child's father.

'Can you prove it?' asked the magistrate.

'My proof is this. I know that he is the father because he has fed and clothed her and has taken trouble to train her in singing and dancing.'

'Is that your proof?' asked the magistrate. 'If I took you in and clothed you, I would be your father?' His tone spoke volumes. He turned to the child and asked her where she would like to go. 'With Mamajee [family name for Miss Warburton Booth],' she said. So the battle was won and the child, the first of many, stayed with them.

People used to ask Miss Warburton Booth who gave her permission to gather children. She would reply 'No one gave me permission. I felt no special call, the need was there and God brought the children in most amazing ways and we were glad to be there to receive them.' In 1926, when she was again at Keswick, as she looked back over the last twelve years since the first child came to be rescued, Miss Warburton Booth was able to say, 'I never in my wildest dreams pictured what has happened.'

Hundreds of little girls and over fifty boys had been

rescued. Women who became Christians and in conse-
quence had been turned out of their homes came to live
with them. They now had twenty-three teachers and
Bible women. They were able to build a new bungalow
and saw, in an amazing way, God providing for their
financial and material needs.

In 1926, they took the step of faith not to accept any
more financial help from ZBMM. They believed that
God's work done in God's way will never lack God's
resources. In 1997, their testimony is that, never asking
anyone or telling anyone but God of their needs, he has
supplied abundantly for the workers and the large family. It is true but costly that 'they who trust Jesus wholly, find him wholly true'.

3

THE EARLY YEARS

It was into this amazingly blessed work that God called Muriel Ainger as a young teacher. It was to be her life work.

Muriel was born in 1903 on the outskirts of Leicester. Her father worked in Railway Insurance. They lived at 402 Narborough Road, Leicester. Muriel was an only child and went to Wyggeston Grammar School from 29th April, 1914 to 19th December, 1921. She met there three girls who were to become lifelong friends, Dorothy Richard, Norah Lloyd and Phyllis Stanley.

Dorothy married Charles Frear, who became a well-known businessman in Leicestershire, later being chairman of the hospital board and Lord Lieutenant of the County. Phyllis and Norah, like Muriel, never married. Phyllis trained as a nurse and became Assistant Matron at the London Hospital. Norah trained as a teacher and later ran her own school in Leicester.

Norah was to have a great influence on Muriel's life. She took her to a Bible Class for girls run on a Sunday afternoon by the Girl Crusaders' Union. The Union had been started by a group of ladies who were concerned with the spiritual welfare of grammar and high school girls, who did not go to Sunday Schools and spent their Sunday afternoons in aimless ways.

Muriel's family were churchgoers and at fourteen she was confirmed in the Church of England. Norah and her other friends at Crusaders were praying for

Muriel, that her confirmation would not be just something routine but that she would come to know Jesus as her own personal Saviour and commit her life to him. To their great joy, this she did at Crusaders.

She was popular at school and good at games. Wyggeston Grammar, now Wyggeston and Queen Elizabeth I College, have records of her being captain of the 1st XI hockey team. She was also Form Captain in the sixth form. She wanted, after she left school, to do Physical Training, but she was turned down as she had a heart murmur, which was not to trouble her until her death in 1995! So she did a Froebel teachers' training course at the Collegiate School, Leicester. She did well and obtained a first class pass in 1925.

At home things were not easy as her mother had developed cancer. After a long and painful illness she died when Muriel was nineteen. Then an aunt came to live with them until she too died some years later.

Mr Ainger subsequently married Jane, a nurse; Muriel and her stepmother became good friends.

Family holidays were spent in Norfolk, for which Muriel developed a lifelong love. During her Froebel training, Muriel began to feel that God was calling her to go for him to India after she had finished her training, but she did not know as yet what work that would be. In the early 1900s, a very remarkable woman, Amy Carmichael, had started a work in South India, in a village called Dohnavur, rescuing children who were sold to the Hindu temples to become brides to the gods. 'Deified sin', Amy Carmichael called it. Muriel's heart and mind were captured by the work among the children there.

The pressure on her spirit was so great that Muriel wrote, applying to go and work with Miss Carmichael in what is still known as the Dohnavur Fellowship.

It was with great eagerness and some trepidation that she waited for Amy Carmichael's reply. This was surely the work for which God had prepared her.

When the long awaited letter arrived from India, she was dismayed and shocked to read that there was no vacancy at Dohnavur for a primary teacher. Politely, but firmly, she was rejected; the door to Dohnavur was shut. Muriel was by now a teacher at a school in Leicester, but was still hoping to go to India. What was God doing? Surely she had heard him aright. Had he not laid the children of India and their need on her heart? What then was he doing?

One of the prayers of Amy Carmichael and the folk at Dohnavur was that God would put the desire in the hearts of other people to start a work of rescuing children in other parts of India.

We cannot be sure how, but perhaps through her links with Norfolk, Muriel came in touch with Elise Page, who had left a very secure, secluded background to go and join Mary Warburton Booth in Gorakhpur. Now Muriel's thoughts and interest began to be turned towards Gorakhpur. She had also heard of the work there, as her great friend Norah Lloyd supported it through the Leicester Girl Crusaders' class, of which Muriel was a member.

In 1926, Mary Warburton Booth came home and went to the Keswick Convention, and to that Convention also went Muriel, where she met Aunt Molly, as Mary Warburton Booth became known.

Aunt Molly, although excited by all God had done and was doing in Gorakhpur, was very conscious of the need for more workers who were called by God to serve the needs of the children of India. So, in God's wonderful way, came about the meeting of these two women of God. Muriel knew that this was the way for her. God wanted her in Gorakhpur.

Amy Carmichael herself first went as a missionary to Japan before going to India to the work God had obviously prepared for her. Both these women could have been discouraged from pursuing God's call on their lives. 1 Peter 1:7 says that the trial of our faith is more precious than gold that perishes. It was their faith that was tried, but they both remained steadfast to God's call and were to come forth as gold. It is how we react to the trials of life that ultimately decides whether we turn out to be inferior plastic or pure gold.

So Muriel had come through this trial of faith and now she was going forward to make her application to the Zenana Bible and Medical Mission under whose auspices the Gorakhpur Fellowship was still operating.

If anyone reading this is facing shut doors, then take heart. God sometimes has seemingly to shut doors, so that we are free to enter other doors that he wants to open for us, as he did for both Muriel and Amy Carmichael.

The Mission had many places where they felt there was need of a Primary teacher. So, when Muriel came before the Mission Society committee, they asked her, 'Are you willing to go anywhere we send you?' Muriel, with a determination which was to characterise her through life, replied, 'Oh no, the Lord has called me to Gorakhpur.'

So, in March 1928, aged twenty-four, Muriel sailed for Gorakhpur.

4

INDIA – FIRST IMPRESSIONS

When Muriel sailed in 1928, India was under British rule. The King appointed a Viceroy to be in charge. There were many British working in India in a variety of jobs; many worked as engineers on the railways, building and running the excellent rail system which still operates in India today. So it was to part of the British Empire that Muriel went.

However, there was much that was different. In India, before partition in 1947, there were Hindus, Muslims and some Buddhists. In many cities the different English denominations had established Christian churches, but Indian Christians were in the minority.

For anyone coming to India for the first time, the extreme poverty hits them. The Mission had a school in Bombay to which Muriel went on her arrival. Under a bridge near the school, she saw people lying on beds consisting only of scrounged newspapers – this was their home.

The long three-day journey from Bombay to Gorakhpur afforded plenty of opportunity for Muriel to see and experience India for the first time – the fascination of the stations, where vendors came to the window shouting *'garam cheea, garam cheea'*, 'hot tea, hot tea', served in earthenware cups, also coffee, puris, chapatis (flat bread), curry, bread (double bread as it is called), fruit, dates etc.; the stalls on the platform selling a wide variety of things such as clothes, socks, shoes, pullovers, hats, pants, sunglasses, briefcases, toys; the richness of the variety of people that is India; the poverty shown by the beggars; the shacks made out of pieces of cardboard and rags built at the side of the road; the rich and ornate palaces and houses; the sheer pressure of people; the noise, the heat, the dirt – this was Muriel's first glimpse of the magic that is India.

She was met at Gorakhpur by Mary Warburton Booth (Aunt Molly) and Elise Page and taken by horse-drawn buggy to the Nurseries buildings just down the road from the station.

It was a relief to come out of the bustle into the high-ceilinged, white bungalow, with its broad verandah at the front, and to meet the Indian workers and children that comprised 'the family'. Aunt Molly had always said God planted them in families. We will not have an institution, we will have a family, she constantly repeated, and on that basis the 'family' had grown.

As Aunt Molly's first task had been to learn the language, so it was with Muriel. She did not find it easy; she had to learn Urdu with its complicated script. Later, after partition, Hindi became the main language spoken in the area. Muriel then taught herself Hindi and had of course to learn a completely different script from the Urdu one she knew. She also started teaching in the Nurseries school and fitting into the life of the family. Mary Warburton Booth writes in her book, *They That Sow*, how God led them to make going out into the villages selling tracts, gospels and Bibles part of the work of the Nurseries families, which it still is today. Muriel went with members of the family into the surrounding villages. She was able to start practising her new language.

Right from the beginning of the Nurseries there was a great desire to go out and tell the people about Jesus and what he had come to do for them. Gorakhpur in those days was not the built-up town it is today and they went through fields and on narrow paths built up between the fields to meet people. That the need was there they had no doubt. One day they met three widows who had been on a fourteen-day pilgrimage into Nepal, where the great god dwelt they said. They had worshipped, paid heavily to the priests and then walked back the fourteen days to Gorakhpur, where they had arrived footsore and weary.

Aunt Molly asked 'Why did you go all that way?' Their swollen, bleeding feet thrust out to rest in front of them were testimony to the painful journey they had made.

'We want salvation,' they said simply, 'and there,' pointing towards the snows, 'our cry is heard by the great god.'

'Do you know the name of the One who gives salvation, who said "Come unto me all you who labour and are heavy laden?" (Matthew 11:28),' Aunt Molly asked.

'No, we have never heard it. What is his name?'

'His name is Jesus.'

So, as so many times in the history of the Nurseries, the wonderful story was told of God becoming the incarnate Jesus, dying on the cross and rising again, giving his Holy Spirit to empower us, that we might know the way of salvation and have the power to live a saved life. When the widows had to go on their journey, they turned back, 'If we forget his name, what shall we do?' they asked. 'He will not forget you,' Aunt Molly said. 'He never forgets.'

'Please write his name on a piece of paper and I will carry it with me wherever I go,' one said. Aunt Molly wrote in Hindi the name of Jesus. 'Yesu, Yesu,' she said. 'He gives salvation.'

How many in the western world will not even go down the road, across the street, to seek salvation, when without cost or suffering we can hear about Jesus.

Although salvation is free, the family learnt that it was probably not good to give tracts completely free.

People value more something they pay for, however little. At the beginning, Aunt Molly gave tracts freely to everyone, but one day she saw a vendor of powder for the eyes and beauty spots, folding the powder into small packets with the paper from the tracts. He felt he had got them freely and should give them freely and they were just the right size to fold for his powders! Others found the 'Way of Salvation' booklet pages were just the right size for making cigarettes!

Therefore it is usual these days to charge a few paisa (pennies) for booklets given. The need is still there, people's hearts and needs have not changed and Jesus is still the only one that can meet that need and satisfy all of our hearts.

So, Muriel in her first years, taught in the school and went out distributing tracts with the evangelising teams. All through her life at the Nurseries she strongly supported this work. She was, in a sense, to the end of her life, an evangelist. She was always keen and looking for opportunity for people to come to know Jesus, but it was not by any means her chief or only gift.

5

NEW EXPERIENCES,
TESTINGS AND BLESSINGS

Muriel was really fitting in and loving her life at the Nurseries. Then the blow fell; she became ill and had to be invalided home before the end of her first term.

It was again a real trial of her faith. She was more sure than ever that Gorakhpur was where God wanted her, but there were months of uncertainty about her health and whether or not she would be able to return to India.

During her time at home, God was very gracious to her and, as she was able to record in her diary in 1987, 'Fifty-three years of the goodness of the Lord. Pentecost Saturday 1934, baptised in the Spirit at Elim Woodlands. Isaiah 60: Arise, shine, for your light has come and the glory of the Lord rises upon you.'

Elim Woodlands was an Elim Bible College in Clapham where Margaret Barbour, a great friend of Muriel's, lived and worked. She went to stay with her, and while she was there, there were special meetings on the work of the Holy Spirit (Acts 1:5; 1 Corinthians 12:13 etc.). During these meetings Muriel felt a pressure on her spirit to go forward to receive the baptism in the Spirit. This was years before the Charismatic Renewal with all the controversy it sadly evoked broke, as it were, on the British Church.

Each night at these meetings the pressure on her spirit got greater, until one night she felt she must go forward. However, as she said later, she felt she just couldn't, as she had on a bright yellow coat; she felt so conspicuous in it and wished she'd worn her grey one. She felt there was no way she could go forward. It is interesting isn't it, what excuses we and the devil can use to keep us from the blessings God wants to give us – in Muriel's case, a yellow coat. In the end, however, her desire for spiritual blessing overcame her self-consciousness. She went forward and received a mighty infilling of the Spirit – she felt immersed in the Spirit – something that never left her all her life.

As a result, she did speak in tongues, but it was never a gift she readily used in public, even though she did from time to time, and interpreted. However, she derived, I know, great blessing through the gift in her time of private prayer and worship.

Muriel had been a great supporter of the Japan Evangelistic Band and one of the tenets of their teaching was 'the second blessing' and 'sanctification'. She had been blessed in earlier years at one of their conferences. Speaking later about the two experiences, she tried to explain the difference as far as she was concerned.

To sanctify, the dictionary says, is 'to set apart for sacred use, to free from sin and evil, to make the means of holiness'. That sanctification experience for her meant setting the direction of her life to be wholly for him and knowing the power in a new way to overcome sin and evil.

'You shall be baptised with the Holy Spirit not many days hence.' The baptism in the Spirit is the filling, the empowering, the anointing of the Spirit for doing the work of Christ. The baptism in the Spirit was a releasing of the Spirit within her heart, a wellspring within her that all through her life gave an upsurging and overwhelming of the Spirit so that she was often completely lost in wonder, love and praise.

Meanwhile in Gorakhpur, Aunt Molly and the others were missing Muriel greatly. She had fitted in so well and was obviously called to the work there. It was a real trial of faith for them as well as for Muriel. Then, in a most unusual way, as God does, he lit a ray of hope in their hearts. The 'family' received parcels of clothes sent to them by friends overseas. Sorting through the clothes, and wondering for whom they would be suitable, Aunt Molly took out a coat, held it up, looked at it and said 'This looks as if it was meant for Muriel, we will keep it for her. I believe this is a token that God is going to send her back to us.'

So it proved to be. Muriel was able to return and, apart from tummy upsets, which most people suffer from time to time in India, she was to have no more real ill health while there. The heart murmur for which she was turned down for Physical Training never troubled her either.

Since she was Froebel trained, her special work was with teaching the toddlers, of whom there was a growing number.

The work among the family too was increasingly occupying her time. It was always a priority with Muriel that every member of the family should come to know Jesus as their personal Saviour and his Lordship in their lives. She put her heart and soul into equipping and training members of the family spiritually, to be able to go out and reach others. Most of the girls went on to marry Christians. They became very real helpers and support in their husband's work, as well as often having their own Christian ministry. They can be found today working in India, Nepal and other lands as keen Christian workers.

Aunt Molly, writing in the 1930s, said, 'Elise [Page] and I concentrated on the compound. Every child must know Jesus, we said to each other, and no woman must miss him here. So we lived and worked and made that our aim. As we worked, others were added to the family month by month until the limited space had burst its bounds, and we built more and watched a family grow up for God.'

Besides the work on the compound and the school, they also went out into the surrounding villages taking simple medicines with them. Every morning they had a crowd of patients and they began with a service in which they sang songs and hymns in Hindi, read and told Bible stories. Writing about this, Aunt Molly said, 'Men and women listened with curiosity but they soon learned where they could get help in their weakness and sickness and were not slow to come to us.' In *They That Sow*, she describes a successful treatment of a man who was cured and how their fame spread like wildfire. The nearest hospital was forty miles away and they longed for skill to tackle more patients. She wrote,

> We prayed with the patients and for them. We told them that the medicine we gave would not help them unless the Lord blessed it. They began to ask for the Jesus medicine, for some who were laid up with high fevers had told their neighbours that two or three doses of the medicine with His Name drove all the fever away. So His Name became as ointment poured forth on the suffering in the villages around.

Although having a dispensary and ministering to the sick has remained part of the work of the Nurseries and Muriel had to be involved in it, it was not something she enjoyed doing. In fact, right up to the end of her life, she did not like any discussion about illness or its symptoms. She said her mother died of cancer but she never spoke of her or about it. It seemed that watching her mother die slowly was such a painful experience for her that talking about any illness later was too painful to bear. If, however, she had to face illness in herself, the Gorakhpur family or among her friends, she steeled herself to cope, but she was always glad if there was someone around who could take responsibility.

With their resources stretched, they felt they could not do more than they were doing. Yet they lifted their eyes to the distant hills of Nepal, a Hindu kingdom, a land closed at that time to outsiders and the gospel.

Muriel, all her life, had a heart for Nepal and, to her great joy, Nepali children were soon being brought to them and they too became part of the family. Aunt Molly writes of their joy when she asked one of the children what she would do when she was big, 'I shall look after children and bring them to Jesus and when I have time I will go out to preach in the villages'.

However, more helpers were needed and Aunt Molly, Elise and Muriel were not satisfied and longed and prayed that 'the Lord of the Harvest would send more labourers'.

These prayers were answered when Rosalind Allen arrived in 1933. Rosalind was to remain a friend of Muriel's for the rest of her life.

6

ROSALIND ALLEN

One of Muriel's gifts was to make and keep friends;
Rosalind Allen was to become one.

Rosalind's background was very different from
Muriel's. Rosalind's mother was a Jacob and traced her
family's associations with India back four generations,
and her cousin, Charles Allen, author of *Plain Tales
From The Raj*, claimed that her father's family's Indian
connection went back to the Battle of Seringa-putam in
1799. Her ancestors included General Jacob of
Jacobabad in Pakistan, and her maternal grandfather,
Colonel S.L. Jacob, who was in the Royal Engineers and
had a name for 'irrigating the Punjab'. Her paternal
grandfather was a director of the newspaper *Pioneer*,
and was an employer of Rudyard Kipling who worked
as a journalist for the paper. Her father's family owned
a leather factory in Cawnpore. Her mother helped
found, in memory of her husband, the Wynberg Allen
Schools in North India, specially to help Anglo Indians.

Rosalind lived with her parents in India until, when
she was twelve, her father, Henry Deacon Allen, died
suddenly of a coronary after walking in the Himalayas.
After his death, Rosalind and her mother and three
younger siblings came home to live in Bath. She suf-
fered an enormous bereavement, not only of her father,
but also of the whole way of life in India. She certainly
left her heart behind there and this drew her to return
later to the country of her childhood. Her younger sister Monica married Dr Geoffrey Lehmann and together

they founded the Herbertpur Christian Hospital, near
Dehra Dun, India, where they worked for over forty
years.

Rosalind was delighted when Aunt Molly, who was
a family friend, invited her to come to the Gorakhpur
Nurseries in 1933. She had hoped to be a doctor, but in
those days it was not thought necessary for young
ladies to have careers. She was, however, able to do a
paramedical course at the Homeopathic Hospital in
London.

In spite of being brought up among the wealthy
Europeans in India, Rosalind had a real love of village
Indians. She longed to go and live among them. All at
the Gorakhpur Nurseries went out on trips to evangelise, but Rosalind wanted to go and stay with the
people for several days or weeks at a time. She longed
not only to take the gospel but also to help the villagers
medically. Her mother was very sympathetic. Rosalind
had seen a caravan in the Punjab which was all fitted up
to enable several people to live in it in the villages; she
was delighted when her mother got one for Gorakhpur.
Rosalind and the Indian helpers went out together in it
to the villages. Sometimes Elise or Muriel went with her
and she enjoyed their trips together.

There were many British stationed in Gorakhpur
and one young lady who worked at the Nurseries used
to go horse riding with a man from one of the regiments
posted there. Miss Warburton Booth did not think he
was at all suitable for her, so Muriel was detailed to go
riding with her each morning. The story has come
down through the years that Muriel successfully
nipped the budding romance in the bud. The lady certainly never married.

There was, however, in the life of Rosalind, a more
determined man. Paul Broomhall had first met
Rosalind when she was at school in Bath and he was at
Monkton Combe School, near Bath. Their two mothers

were great friends. Paul's parents, Dr and Mrs
Broomhall, were in China, so they naturally asked their
great friend Mrs Allen to invite their son out from
school. Paul first fell in love with Rosalind when he was
about thirteen as they were climbing together through a
window onto a roof, in order to hide from some friends
in a party game! He decided from then on that Rosalind
was the girl he was going to marry. He made several
abortive attempts to persuade her to marry him, but
Rosalind was determined to return to India. Paul
trained as a chartered surveyor and when established in
business he decided to pursue his fair Rosalind.

When in 1937 he discovered that Rosalind was coming home on a boat, the *Viceroy of India*, he was determined to get a berth on the boat and be with her on the
trip home. He told Mrs Allen of his intentions. She was
concerned for him and her daughter, and wrote to tell
Rosalind so in a letter she received on her arrival in
Bombay. 'My precious Rosalind, Paul told me on the
eve of his departure that he was sailing to Bombay. It
was such a shock and I know it will be to you. I tried to
dissuade him from such a step but he had made up his
mind and would not change. I have never seen or heard
of such persistency. He certainly must love you very
deeply and truly. I do not know what you will say to
him. You must have met him by the time you read this
and I suppose you have either to say that once and for
all you have finished with him – or that you will marry
him. It must be one or the other.'

Paul in the meantime was trying to get a berth on the
boat. Things were complicated by the fact that the
Viceroy himself was travelling with his entourage and
Paul was told there was no available passage for him.
He persisted in his efforts to get a berth, however, and
was eventually given one, in the Viceroy's party, as one
member did not turn up!

So they had the voyage home together from Bombay

to England. Paul Broomhall, who was a great raconteur, enjoyed telling his granddaughters the story of how the captain of the ship fancied Rosalind himself and when the ship docked at Port Said he told Paul that Rosalind had disembarked and booked a berth on another ship, in order to escape Paul's pursuit. Paul was just about to dash off to the shipping office to see if he could transfer his passage to the other ship when he decided to check Rosalind's cabin. On finding all her clothes still hanging in the wardrobe, he realised he had almost been the victim of a hoax. The voyage on the *Viceroy of India* continued and by the time they got home, Rosalind had agreed to marry Paul and he gave her an engagement ring. A photo of Rosalind on deck with the captain survives to this day.

However, after she got home she began to have doubts and returned the ring to Paul. He sent it back and she returned it again. Paul decided there was nothing he could do but 'watch and pray'. He apparently begged God to help him to 'leave off loving Rosalind if he was not meant to have her'.

Imagine his joy when, after about a year of waiting, he got a phone call from Rosalind to say she was on holiday in the Isle of Wight, but was coming up to London to see the dentist and would he meet her. He immediately arranged to do so, outside the Army and Navy Stores in Victoria Street.

When he arrived, Rosalind was standing at the entrance nearest Victoria Station. He immediately bundled her into a taxi. He told the taxi driver to drive where he liked until told to stop and he would pay him. As soon as they were in the taxi, he said to Rosalind, 'Do you want to marry me or not?' 'Yes, Paul, I do, but what about mother?' Mrs Allen, although she liked Paul, really hoped that Rosalind would marry, not a business man, but a missionary.

'You leave your mother to me,' said Paul and told

the taxi driver to drive to St Paul's Church, Portman Square. There he asked his old friend, Colin Kerr, to get him a special licence to marry Rosalind the following Wednesday. He then took Rosalind down to Mrs Allen. She was most surprised when they walked in together. 'Whatever are you doing here, Paul?' she asked. 'Mrs Allen,' he replied, 'we have come to ask you to our wedding next Wednesday.'

After the initial shock, and realising there was little she could do to change things, Mrs Allen capitulated. She said to Rosalind, 'Well, we must go to London tomorrow and get your wedding clothes.'

So Paul and Rosalind Broomhall were married at St Paul's Church, Portman Square in September 1938.

Rosalind never lost her heart for mission and in later years was never happier than when making trips back to India and, when it opened, to Nepal. One who had been a child when she was at the Nurseries, Kamolini, even after they both married, remained one of Rosalind's special friends to the end of her life. You can read more of Kamolini in Chapter 13.

In some ways the villages of India remained Rosalind's first love. Muriel remembered how on her last visit back to them before she died, Rosalind turned to Paul and said, 'Oh Paul, why did you marry me, I could have stayed here if you hadn't.'

Rosalind had a man who adored her and whom she loved dearly, a son and daughter, a beautiful home and everything she could want. Muriel had none of those things which are counted to be the most coveted and yet she was fully satisfied being single and, in a sense, burying herself in the back of beyond in India.

It is, however, certain that both women and Paul have now heard their Lord say, 'Well done, my good and faithful servants' (Matthew 25:21).

Rosalind was on the Personnel Committee and Paul on the Executive Committee, and later chairman of the

Missionary Fellowship, now called Interserve, through
all its changes of name, Zenana Bible and Medical
Mission, Bible and Medical Missionary Fellowship,
then BMMF. Altogether, the years they served the mission added up to 110 years between them. No one will
ever know what their support and help has meant, not
just to the Gorakhpur Nurseries, but to many missions,
nationals and missionaries.

Interserve certainly greatly benefited from Paul's
wisdom and financial acumen over the years. Even in
the year he died, 1995, he enabled Interserve to balance
their books with the legacy he left them. He was wor-
ried sometimes that people had a romantic idea that
being called to the mission field was the highest calling.
Whereas, he felt that those with business ability to
make money should consider whether God was not
challenging them to stay and support missions, so that
many others might go. He wanted all to be very sure of
their call, to go or to stay. Interestingly, this was a decision that his own wife found hard.

Rosalind died in 1986 and Paul's feelings about her
to the end are expressed in a tiny etching in one of the
glass panes in the Memorial Window in the church at
Penshurst, East Sussex – 'the unfading beauty of a gen-
tle and quiet spirit'.

7

SISTER THILDE

With Rosalind leaving and subsequently getting married, the Nurseries were again in need of new personnel.

In 1937 Aunt Molly went on leave to London. At the China Inland Mission in Newington Green, she met Sister Annie, an Englishwoman belonging to the Friedenshort Sisters, who invited her to come to take meetings in Friedenshort, which at that time was based in Upper Silesia near the German–Polish border.

Aunt Molly was pleased to go, but as she could not speak German, an interpreter was needed. Sister Thilde Gaupp was chosen. She was thrilled at the thought of meeting Mary Warburton Booth. Sister Thilde, like Muriel, was a trained primary teacher and like Muriel had applied to Dohnavur and been turned down as they said they were not in need of a teacher. However, on the day Aunt Molly arrived in Friedenshort for her visit, Sister Thilde heard that her mother was ill. It was very sad for her, both that her mother was ill and that she would not have the opportunity to translate for Aunt Molly.

Thilde went home to her mother, who died three days later. Thilde got back to Friedenshort the night before Aunt Molly was leaving. It was late, but Thilde felt she wanted to meet her. Aunt Molly was already in bed when Thilde knocked on her door. On a cheery 'Come in', Sister Thilde went in. It was to be a never-to-be-forgotten moment. To Thilde's surprise, on entering,

Aunt Molly sat up in bed and held her hands out to her, took both of Thilde's hands in hers, and looking straight into her eyes said, 'My dear, God has given you to us hasn't he?' Thilde, recounting it said, 'I just said yes'.

It was a 'yes' of commitment, as Thilde was to stay for over fifty years at the Gorakhpur Nurseries and became one of Muriel's best and trusted friends. She arrived in 1938 and like Muriel was at once plunged into learning Hindi.

A plot of land, five miles from the city of Gorakhpur, had been taken by Mama Ji (as Aunt Molly was known in the family) in 1936, as an overflow for the family in Gorakhpur both for holidays and a place of retreat. They called it then, as they do today, Jainager (place of victory).

In 1938, Muriel moved out to be in the newly-built Zion Cottage in Jainagar. All their buildings and places of work were given biblically-related names, such as Zion, Jerusalem, Peace Cottage, Bethany, Bethlehem. Thilde (or Bahin Ji as she became known) went with her along with fourteen children, seven schoolgirls up to twelve years old and seven pre-school children. They had no Bua (older sister – an Indian helper in charge of a 'family' within the fellowship) with them at first. Muriel was to be in charge there for all the rest of her years in Gorakhpur.

The pattern of the work in both places was, and still is, 'God sets the solitary in families', not a Home but home where all would live as a family. The girls as they grow up can say what they feel God is calling them to. Most want to get married and for these, marriages are arranged, while others may choose to stay on and look after the family. They may, on leaving school, take care of one child, then bit by bit each gathers around her an increasing number of children, until a Bua in her thirties has in her little family group a wide range of ages.

Later some Buas with their families moved out to Jainager to be with Muriel.

Muriel was always very keen on gardening and horticulture, so at Jainagar she developed the land and garden. The aim was to make the family self-supporting as far as vegetables were concerned. Muriel became very skilled in this work. They also had a school and it was to help with this Thilde went out to join Muriel. There were daily prayers and Bible teaching and, as soon as she learnt the language, Thilde became very adept in this. She was able to make the most wonderful visual aids.

During the first year of her stay, the world outside Gorakhpur was getting anxious about the advance of Hitler into other countries. Just after Thilde arrived in Gorakhpur, Neville Chamberlain went to Munich to see Adolf Hitler and they signed a Peace Treaty. Neville Chamberlain returned to England to say that the war, which many feared might be imminent because of Hitler's activities, had been averted. It was however a very uneasy peace that ensued in 1939. It was not easy for Thilde, as a German with only English colleagues in India, which was then still under the British Raj.

As we know, on 3rd September, 1939, Britain declared war on Germany. Thilde was immediately, as far as the authorities were concerned, considered an enemy alien. The order came that she was to be interned. Aunt Molly went to see the British authorities and promised to be responsible for her for as long as the war should last. This meant that Thilde had to be under her direct authority and return to live in Gorakhpur; she was not allowed to go out from the Nurseries' Gorakhpur property (even to Jainagar) for over six years. When it was decided that Thilde would be allowed to stay in Gorakhpur, a British official came to see all was well. He asked Thilde if she had a camera and when she said she had, he told her, 'Well, get rid of it! Sell it'. So Muriel bought Thilde's camera for five rupees.

As far as the others were concerned she had joined the family and was one of them. 'We are all one in Christ' was their motto. It was however not easy for any of them. When Hitler turned against the Jews, Thilde found this very difficult indeed. I had not realised how deeply it had affected her, until years later. In the 1970s Muriel and I talked of joining a party going from India to Israel and I suggested Thilde come with us. When I asked her, to my amazement her eyes filled with tears and she walked quickly away from me, saying, 'Oh, I could never go to Israel after what my people did to the Jews.'

It was good she was with children who did not realise the meaning and full significance of the war. They loved her and she became the confidante of many of them. Over the years she increasingly became the oil of the Fellowship. Muriel and the others could on occasions, without ever realising it, be very autocratic and British Rajish. Thilde had great sensitivity and could see what was happening in situations and she would then tactfully move in and smooth things over. I have seen Muriel be brisk, insensitive and almost rude when faced with a situation she did not want to be involved in, or of which she did not approve, whereas even in these circumstances, Thilde would act with love, grace and understanding. She was a tremendous support and help to Muriel over the years, who regarded her probably as her closest friend.

Thilde showed that characteristic devotion to duty that marked all from overseas, as they did not come to do a job, but to be part of a family, which is a lifetime commitment, and they took names that gave them a family connection. Aunt Molly was Mama Ji (mother) Elise Page, Mausi Ji, but Mata Ji after Aunt Molly died. Muriel was Phuphu Ji (aunt), Thilde, Bahin Ji (sister)

and Miss Ivy Hill, who arrived in 1946, Dadi Ji (grannie
– because of her white hair) and Elise Page's niece, Dr
Rosemary Page, who arrived in 1952, Khala Ji (a
younger aunt). It is Rosemary who is now in charge of
the work.

8

CHANGES AND ADJUSTMENTS

By the time Sister Thilde had her first leave in 1948, great changes had taken place. Aunt Molly had died in 1945 and had handed over the leadership of the Fellowship to her trusted friend and colleague, Elise Page, who then became known as Mata Ji (mother of the family). Retiring by nature, it was a real step of faith for her to take on the leadership. She had also lost a much loved friend. She had a very strong bond with Muriel, who was her second in command, but Muriel lived at Jainagar, five miles away, and then went on leave to England in 1946.

Meanwhile, in England, a Miss Ivy Hill was running a Nursing Home in Clapham. She belonged to the local church, where she had a very good relationship with the vicar and his wife, even going on holiday with them but, almost unbeknown to herself, she was seeking for something deeper than she found there.

One Sunday she wanted to go to a Communion Service at 12 noon after her duties in the Nursing Home. She rang round the local churches and the only place she could find where there was a service at that time was a local mission hall. Telling the story years later, she told how she had gone there in a fur coat (they were good dress wear in those days) and her jewellery. As she sat among the obviously poorer people at the mission hall she felt very superior to them. However, as the service went on, she was grabbed by something as she had never been before. So much so, that she decided to go back for the evening service. She recounted how her Nursing Home staff thought she had gone crackers. However, to the evening service she went, again in her fur coat and jewellery, and again feeling very superior. As she sat there in that mission hall, which had previously been a swimming bath, she said a ray of light came down from an upper window onto the rail at the front. Then, to her amazement, she saw a shining figure come down the ray of light. The figure stopped and put his hands on the rail. Ivy Hill said that, as she looked at the figure, he turned over his hands and she saw that they had nail prints in them and she cried out – 'It's Jesus'. He looked at her and said, 'Come unto Me'. She said she suddenly felt mean and dirty and took off her jewellery and the rings on her fingers and stuffed them into her coat pockets.

She had to rush off at the end of the service to be back on duty, but as she was leaving she asked the two in charge of the mission hall, 'What time are you up until? I must come back and talk to you'. 'Oh, if it's something to do with your soul, anytime,' they replied. So she went back to talk to them later that evening and was, in her own words, 'gloriously converted that night'. Shortly afterwards she was baptised by immersion.

She then began to feel that God had new plans for her life. She had always run the Nursing Home with her mother, but when her mother died and the Nursing Home was bombed during the war, she decided to give it up.

She longed to do something for the Lord. She felt she had wasted years of her life just being a 'churchgoer' and not really understanding the need to know Christ as her own Saviour and have a personal relationship with him. Joel 2:25 speaks of the Lord restoring the years the locust have eaten. In her new burning zeal for the Lord, she longed to make up for the years when she had largely just lived for herself. The need overseas was brought to her notice, particularly by a friend who also lived in Clapham and was secretary of the North India Mission.

She started to pray for the babies born in the Nursing Home, that some would go overseas for the Lord. I don't know how many did, but she was my mother's midwife and I went to Nepal from 1957 to 1989 and Doreen Grimes, who was also one of 'her' babies, spent seventeen years in India and Nepal.

Then Matie (as she was called) realised she should not just pray for others to go. She should go herself. So she decided to go and visit the workers in her friend's North India Mission, and visit Gorakhpur, as she also knew of the Nurseries. She travelled round North India and early in 1946 arrived at the Nurseries. She said later that, as she walked up the drive, she again saw the figure of Jesus, this time standing on the outside verandah of the Nurseries, welcoming her. She at once felt at home and knew that this was where the Lord wanted her to stay.

Elise Page, in her loneliness, welcomed her and felt that she was the one that God had sent into her life to be her friend and companion. Although on matters of leadership Elise could be very firm, she was basically timid and shy while Matie was adventurous and positive, so in that way they were a good combination.

Matie's coming was not easy for Muriel, however. Matie spent more and more time with Elise, and Muriel felt it was impossible to continue her friendship with Elise as it had been before. It seems that even saints have problems with relationships. It is, in a sense, not what happens to us in life that makes us what we are but how we handle it. Muriel had to work very hard over the years with her feelings about the arrival of Ivy Hill.

Matie was older than the others when she came to

the Nurseries. While she did make an attempt to learn Hindi, she could not manage it. She found listening and hearing the sounds difficult. The girls, although they understood some English, were reluctant to speak it, so Elise and the others had to constantly act as interpreters. Elise wrote of Matie in 1948, 'Miss Hill came to us as a visitor and felt the Lord's leading to stay on. A woman of wide experience, she loves the family and does much to help us in many ways, trains the girls who look after our cooking and house, has an eye to the motor expeditions to the villages. She will also help (being a nurse) with the Jainager dispensary. She understands prayer; the Lord blesses that ministry.'

In a spiritual community, even being very spiritual can be irritating at times! I knew Matie could be trying when, for instance, she decided to have a long grace or sing the Hallelujah chorus just when Muriel had made a particularly delicious soufflé. She was very generous and tended to buy more than was needed – as for example, when I was in Nepal, she bought me a much needed kerosene stove. However, for some reason she felt she should buy me two, which I did not need. When I told Muriel, she said, 'Oh, Matie's motto is, never buy one if six will do'.

So Matie arrived and became grist to Muriel's mill. She stayed for twenty-six years from 1946 until she retired home with Elise Page in 1972.

It was never a situation that Muriel found easy, but probably Muriel would not have become the understanding woman she was if she had not had to cope with her own relationship battle. I am not sure that Matie realised how trying she was to Muriel. She tended to dominate situations she was in and not be very sensitive to how people were reacting to her 'take over'.

Anyone coming in would never have known there was any tension. Thilde often acted as a defuser! Matie at the end of her life, after Elise had died, left the house in which they lived in Blakeney, Norfolk, to Muriel and Thilde . . . but that comes later.

After Matie died in October 1980, Muriel wrote

Miss Hill had a great love for each one in the family and took great interest in their affairs. Her wide experience in nursing and with babies was a great help and her advice much valued. Outside the family she had a wide ministry among English speaking people in Gorakhpur itself and in other places. Many were blessed and came to know the Lord through her witness. This continued in England. Miss Hill had a caring love for people, an intense desire that each one should find that all needs are met in Jesus. She herself had a definite spiritual experience late in life and this gave her a particular understanding of the problems of others. Many will remember her with gratitude.

9

HOME LEAVE

Muriel had been in Gorakhpur all through the Second
World War, from 1939 to 1945. Safe passages home
were extremely difficult to get, but in 1946 Muriel managed to get a berth on a troop ship. A very uncomfort-
able journey it was, but Muriel was grateful to have it
and to be going home to see her father and friends.

Her father by this time was married to Jane, who
became a good friend of Muriel's. They were living in
Leicestershire and it was that area that Muriel considered home. Many of her Leicester friends had kept in
touch. She was an excellent letter-writer and although,
because of pressure of work, they tended to be rare, her
letters when received were much appreciated and often
kept.

Her good friend, Norah Lloyd, was running the
GCU class in Leicester and they were strong supporters
of the Nurseries which sent out a regular newsletter to
prayer partners and supporters. Many took on particular young people to pray for. This became, for many of
them, a lifetime commitment, which is still going on.
Norah Lloyd was for many years the distribution secretary of the newsletter and the link with the prayer partners and supporters.

Muriel's friend, Phyllis, had moved away to follow
her nursing profession, but it was always a great joy to
both of them when they were able to meet. Her school
friend, Dorothy, was now married to Charles Frears, a
very successful business man. It was lovely to go to her

beautiful home and meet her again with her husband
and children.

For Muriel there was much news to catch up on.
England was still on rationing (there had been rationing
in India too) and its people were recovering from six
years of war, losing loved ones and, in some cases, having their homes bombed. Muriel enjoyed renewing all
these contacts and making new friends. She was always
so interested in people and such a good listener that
people quickly confided in her and regarded her as a
friend. She was, however, very strong-minded and per-
ceptive and could not be put upon in any way, though
this was not always apparent to people at first. She travelled round the country taking meetings in places
where there were prayer supporters.

Muriel, from the time she was converted, kept in
close touch with the Girl Crusaders Union. She first
attended one of their camps in 1927, before she went to
India. Ruth Germain, who was a girl at a camp at which
Muriel was an officer, speaks of the great spiritual
impact she made at the camp and on her own life.

While she was home in 1947, she was invited by
Norah Lloyd as a missionary speaker at a Girl Crusader
houseparty of which Norah was commandant. It was
there I first met Muriel, and she made a lasting impression on me, as she did on many people. She was a good
speaker, and from the beginning, in a way before her
time, used visual aids, such as the sari she wore, to illus-
trate her talks.

Muriel was also interested in the Japan Evangelistic
Band, so she went to their conference at High Leigh,
Hoddesdon in Hertfordshire, where she met and made
many friends.

She then went to Wales, where the Bible College of
Wales and its leader, Rees Howells, and the staff there
became friends and supporters of the Nurseries over
the years, feeling a mutual rapport with them as they

are run on similar faith lines. The Nurseries also had many friends in Eire and Northern Ireland and Muriel visited them too. Being a teacher, she kept in touch with what was going on in the teaching world, and she went to the Teachers' Prayer Bond (which was absorbed into Christians in Education) conference.

Her good friend, Margaret Barbour, was still living in the Elim Bible College in Clapham. However, shortly after the war she felt God was leading her to buy property in Eastbourne, to run as a guest house and a place where people could come for spiritual refreshment. This she did and was later joined there by Vera Hawkins. Muriel later really enjoyed her visits to Queen's Gardens, just opposite the pier in Eastbourne; she had a great love for the sea, going on it or just sitting looking at it.

Muriel had been baptised in the Spirit while with Margaret in 1934. They had kept in touch by letter and now found wonderful fellowship together in the Spirit. In the intervening years, they had both gone through very different experiences. In Gorakhpur, they were further away from the theological arguments that surrounded the subject of baptism in the Spirit than Margaret was. However, they were not without those who murmured about them. I remember being told, in hushed tones, as if it meant they were peculiar, that the people at the Nurseries spoke in tongues. Muriel was always, all through her life, grateful for that experience, though she never forced it on others. She felt, I know, that 'the baptism' adds a plus and release to any Christian's life.

Muriel rejoiced in being home and seeing what new books had been published. All through her life she liked to keep up to date. She read widely and got book lists sent to Gorakhpur, and having perused them, ordered the ones that she felt would be helpful for herself and the others to read, so they got a regular supply of new books. She could in this way keep up to date with what was going on in the Christian Church world-wide. She loved biographies, autobiographies and good stories. She had all the Miss Read and Elizabeth Goudge books, for example. She did not like detective stories or murders like Agatha Christie's novels, though we did manage to persuade her to read her autobiography!

One of her characteristics, right to the end of her life, was her openness to consider new ideas and to change. In some things, however, she would not change, whatever the modern trends might be. For instance, she remained a complete teetotaller to the end. She had seen so much social poverty caused by drink. She believed that one drop of alcohol could impair people's judgement and ability. Also she deplored the amount of money uselessly spent on it. She could see no reason for drinking and was sad when she came home to see the extent to which alcohol was increasingly drunk in England and the relaxed attitudes of Christians to it.

Incidentally, it is interesting that the newly emerging church in Nepal made it a rule that baptised believers do not drink alcohol. It has been such a menace there. There is a very potent brew made from rice, called rakshi, which many, particularly the men, drank to excess and would often get drunk and beat their wives. The new women converts, asked what was one of the nicest things about their families becoming Christian, would say, 'Oh, our husbands don't beat us now'.

Muriel had to face a difficult change when she got back to the Nurseries after her months at home. Aunt Molly was no longer there, Elise Page was now the leader and with her was the newcomer, Ivy Hill.

10

NEW INDIA – FACING CHANGE

When Muriel returned, she went back to be in charge in Jainager. Thilde was in Gorakhpur and Ivy Hill was increasingly becoming Elise Page's constant companion. Muriel at Jainager had Marian Paint to help her, she had been lent from another Society. Marian stayed for twenty years but never actually became a member of the Fellowship.

In 1948, Muriel became Secretary of the Nurseries Fellowship which involved increased office work. It was a post she was to hold until 1987.

To support them in the work in India, the Gorakhpur Nurseries had a Board of Trustees; well-known and trusted members of the Christian community, such as Dr Ben Wati (Secretary of the Evangelical Fellowship of India), Dr Victor Manogarom (Youth for Christ Director) and Rev Subodh Sahu (a well-known evangelist). Every year, in November, these men came with others for the Trustees meetings. These times were always a rededication of themselves and the work to God. They were blessed too by the spiritual input of such men to the family. For instance, Rev Gladwin Das of the Scripture Union came and took a Vacation Bible School for all, teaching the teachers and Buas how to lead. Elise wrote, 'The school children were thrilled with the classes and the test at the end which they all passed!'

Elise wrote of Muriel in 1948, 'She has been here twenty years. Froebel-trained she started off with a

class of toddlers, now grown and helping. She looks
after all at Jainagar, five miles out of Gorakhpur and
has grappled manfully with the rationing business for
the whole company and is in every way a tower of
strength.' (During and after the war there was rationing
in India.)

That people should be well fed was one of the tenets
of Muriel's life. The food at the Nurseries for the west-
erner was mainly western. It was an environment in
which they felt they could function best and the food
that helped them to stay healthy and be committed to
the people they were called to serve. Muriel, to the end,
loved her English afternoon tea and it was a feature too
of her Gorakhpur life. Although later on she had others,
whom she had taught to cook, cooking for her, she
always took a keen interest in the ordering of food and
the way it was cooked. I benefited when I was in Nepal.
Often when working in the hills in isolated places we
did not have much variety in food. Muriel used to lay
on special treats when I came to Gorakhpur. Dr Rose
Page said one day, 'You needn't think we eat like this
all the time'. Muriel, however, made sure, whenever
and however possible, they had a good diet. Although
very spiritual, hers was not a head in the clouds spiri-
tuality, it was based in the realities of daily living. She
had no time for humbug in life and if she heard of anything of which she did not approve, after listening, she
could sometimes be heard to say – something which
people just meeting her casually would think was very
unlikely – that the situation was 'spitworthy'. On other
occasions, it could be 'weepworthy'.

Spitworthy or weepworthy, the ladies at the
Nurseries around this time had lived through some
traumatic changes. In 1947 British rule ceased and India
became a democratic and independent nation. This
meant that the British were no longer part of the ruling
class. Although there had been riots in Gorakhpur, the

folk at the Nurseries had survived, as they were well-known and the rescue work they were doing was respected.

It was however a tremendous change. They had to get visas to stay and work in India and to obtain these became increasingly difficult as the years went by. Still today, residential permits have to be renewed annually. Although they had given their lives to the Indians, they were a product of the British Raj. Muriel wore a sari and continued to do so even when she came to England to retire at the end of her life, but she never ceased to be British. She actually tried hard to 'become Indian'. For about twenty years she did not return to England, so as not to break her residence in India. She thereby hoped to have a better chance to get Indian citizenship. Indian members of the Trust went with her many times to offices in Delhi and Lucknow to plead her case. There is a fat file in the Nurseries with records of her application. It was a sad day when Rose Page, going to the local CID office on her own business, was handed a note for Muriel. It read: 'You are not considered a fit person for Indian citizenship'. The reason was probably political or maybe religious. She was, above all, a missionary.

In England, when people talk of the British Raj, the impression often given is that nothing good came out of it. Travelling round India and hearing many Indians talking, who were there at the time, it was apparently not all bad. Many spoke with tears in their eyes of the wonderful sahibs they had known and loved who were good to them as no one else had been. The railway itself had been the work of British engineers. We know that Rosalind Allen's uncle had irrigated the Punjab – many places in the world today are still without irrigation.

As it was a big adjustment for the Indians to take over government and authority in the offices, so it was for the ladies to adjust to the new regime. Since Muriel

was Secretary, there was a lot of adjusting in her work
to be done.

What helped was that they all really loved India and
the Indians, though they found the increased delays
and red tape trying. Muriel would say, when things
were most frustrating, 'Well, this is our beloved
Hindustan.'

11

THE FIRST DOCTOR

The British Raj was a thing of the past by the time the next recruit came along. Dr Rosemary Page had known of the work in Gorakhpur since childhood, through her aunt, Elise. But when Rosemary in her late teens knew herself to be called and took up medicine with the mission field in view, she had to be extra sure of her destination. 'I suppose you will go to India to join your aunt?' enquired well-meaning friends. 'No, I won't! Why should I?' was the cross reply, and she began to make enquiries about Japan.

But during the medical course in Edinburgh the need in the Nurseries came before her again. For Rosemary, the question was, 'If God is calling me to Gorakhpur, I might have to run a hospital on faith lines! Can I? But if HE is calling me, of course I can!' This was corroborated by 1 Timothy 6:17: 'Trust not in uncertain riches, but in the living God, who gives richly all things to enjoy.'

Rosemary wrote to her aunt telling her how the Lord had been speaking to her – it was her letter of application. Back came the answer from Elise by return of post, 'Hallelujah! Aunt Molly knew years ago that you would be coming but we couldn't say anything until you yourself knew!' That was her letter of acceptance.

Five more years of preparation passed as Rosemary finished her medical course, gained hospital experience as a house officer and had two years' missionary training at Redcliffe College, Chiswick.

At last, in 1952, Rosemary arrived in Gorakhpur. She was the first doctor they had had and she had her own problems in adjusting. She was thrilled, though, that there was a possibility of helping in the new work that the Nurseries were hoping to start in Nepal.

Muriel had a great love for Nepal and the Nepalis. She often told how they pioneered all along the Nepal frontier and met the trains at the little faraway railway stations, talking with the passengers and selling Gospel portions, and many were the thrilling experiences they had. They were swayed and rocked across country in the roughest of bullock carts but it was worth it, she said. Nepal was always dear to the hearts of all the folk at the Gorakhpur Nurseries. Over the years they were always thrilled when Nepali children joined them, as in 1950 when Elise Page wrote of seven little Nepali girls being added to the family and of the possibility of another one coming. Earlier in the month one had come, so ill, with the largest spleen the doctor had ever seen; it was feared she might not live – but she did! She grew up to marry a Nepali and go to work with him in Nepal. Sadly he died young, of cancer, leaving her a widow with two children, who are, however, at the time of writing, still living and working in Nepal.

Nepal was for many years a closed land, so it was with great excitement that Elise Page wrote in February 1951, 'The greatest thrill of all in the outside work is that we have been in Nepal'. A revolution was taking place there at that time and they were not sure if they would be able to go, as there had been fighting, but when they heard that the king of Nepal had returned to Kathmandu and the fighting was over, they decided to go. In 1951, the king, with the help of friends in India, led a coup to free himself and his land. Previously he had been virtually a prisoner in his own palace, kept there by the ruling Ranas. Nepal is a Hindu kingdom (the only one in the world) and the Ranas are one of the higher castes within Hinduism. From this time on Nepal was open to outsiders and to the gospel, but preaching was not allowed. Those who went in could practise as Christians, but it was (and still is in 1997) against the law to convert anyone or to change your religion. However, the Bible (or the Good Book as we called it) says that 'we should be ready always to give an answer to every man that asks us the reason for the hope in us' (1 Peter 3:15) and as people asked lots of questions, the gospel spread. According to Nepali law, everyone should follow the traditions of their forefathers, so, for example, if you were born a Hindu you should remain a Hindu, if born a Moslem, remain a Moslem.

In February 1951, a party of twelve set out from Gorakhpur with twenty-one bags filled with 130 books each, and a tin box of spare Christian literature. They had the promise of God from Deuteronomy 9:1, 3: 'Thou art to pass over Jordan [which for them meant the border of Nepal] this day, to go in to possess nations greater and mightier than thyself, cities great and fenced up to heaven . . . Understand therefore this day, that the Lord thy God is he which goeth over before thee' (AV).

At 6.00 a.m. in the half light they set forth. When they came to the first village, six stayed behind and had a grand day working there and in an adjoining village, preaching and selling large numbers of gospels and tracts. The rest of them proceeded further, not knowing at first that they were actually a few miles over the border and, to their great delight, in Nepal. They wrote,

Eight villages in Nepal were reached by the Good News that day, four hundred Christian books and six New Testaments sold and what a ready hearing we had. How eagerly they bought the books. A lad wanted so much to buy a New Testament. He emp-

tied his pockets of all he had and though it was not
the full amount, how could he be refused? A lad in a
village in the Closed Land!

Two of the 'girls' took off their sandals and stepped into
the water – they were claiming for the Lord that it
might become a place for baptism and that multitudes,
who usually did their puja (worship of idols) there,
might find the Lord and worship and follow Him.

How much we who entered the land after 1951 owe
to those people who, like the Gorakhpur Nurseries,
claimed the land for us. There has certainly been an
amazing number of people turning to Christ, until
Nepal is now (1997) the second fastest growing church
in the world. When Elise was writing in 1951 there was
no known church nor any known believers.

So, when Rosemary arrived in 1952, there was much
talk and planning about going to Nepal. They wanted if
possible to have work over the border there. In 1951,
Nepal had opened to outsiders, and others, like their
friends Hilda Steele and Dr Lily O'Hanlon, had begun
to pioneer the work of the International Nepal
Fellowship in Pokhara, Nepal, known first as the
Nepali Evangelistic Band, then Nepal Evangelistic
Band, then NEB, later changed to the INF.

But it was not until 1954 that the dream was fulfilled. After much prayer, thought and planning, a
group of seven from the Nurseries had the joy of going
over the border into Nepal. They trundled along the
primitive rutted roads in an old Ford van, looking for
somewhere to settle and start work, but having no idea
where. Suddenly, on one of the primitive tracks, their
vehicle sprung a leak. It meant the driver walking back
to the border, twelve or so miles, and then taking the
bus to Gorakhpur – and an enforced encampment for
the ladies, which lasted for three weeks.

However, during that time, they made friends with

the local officials, the happy outcome being that they were given land for a dispensary. The transaction was duly signed and witnessed. They had arrived!

The first hut of mud and grass walls, with a thatched roof supported by wood and bamboo poles, was soon erected. There the dispensary functioned. By Easter 1955, a larger house was ready for occupation. One end was used as the dispensary and the other was lived in by the team. A separate hut was then dedicated as a House of Prayer, and a Communion Service was held there on Easter Sunday. Five of the Gorakhpur Nurseries Buas moved out to run it. Much of the supervision and initial running of the work was done by Dr Rosemary Page.

The little plot of land became known to the people round it as God's Garden. This was because of two things that happened early on. The first concerned an outbreak of fire in the nearby vicinity of the new mud-and-straw-built medical dispensary. The people who lived in the surrounding huts of similar construction were leaving their homes and frantically trying to rescue their meagre possessions. They urged the Gorakhpur girls in charge of the dispensary to do likewise, but to their astonishment, one of them replied calmly that God, whose building it was, would protect it. They remained calm and stayed put. Amazement turned to awe when the wind suddenly changed and although most, if not all, of the surrounding houses were reduced to ashes, the dispensary remained unscarred. The fire had actually come so close that the foliage by the boundary fence was seared. Seeing this, the villagers surmised that there was a Power in charge of the dispensary and its workers and the lives of the team in their midst inclined them to regard the Power as friendly. The trickle of patients coming for medical treatment now became a stream.

The second happening was late one night when

some people, approaching the dispensary garden intending to help themselves to the produce, saw something which made them beat a hasty retreat. At the gateway stood a figure in white which they took for its guardian angel. When a friendly neighbour told the story at the dispensary, it was definitely established that no member of the team had been abroad that night.

The work and blessing in the dispensary grew. As it was becoming increasingly difficult for Dr Rose to live and work in two places, the work was more and more run by the buas, but they longed and prayed for trained staff, as the medical and spiritual work there increased.

12

GOD'S GARDEN, NEPAL

The work developed in God's Garden and there was felt the need for a doctor there. Elise Page and Ivy Hill had met a Scottish doctor, Agnes Gilruth, and they met again when they were in England. When Agnes heard of the need in God's Garden, she felt God was calling her.

As all the Nurseries' work was run on faith lines, looking only to God to supply their needs, Elise told Agnes that she should be prepared to trust God to provide all her travelling expenses. This would increase her faith for the way God would undertake for her in the future. Agnes said, 'God knew my faith was small', but within two weeks she received a cheque for £500 from an elderly cousin of her father's, whom she had not met for years, with an accompanying note to say she wanted her to spend it now and not keep it in the bank.

That money paid not only all her expenses out to Gorakhpur but left enough to buy in a whole lot of drugs for the dispensary. That, she said, was the beginning of her living on faith lines – letting only God know her needs. This continued and all her needs and the helpers she worked with have been abundantly supplied. As she said, 'God is faithful who promised'.

Elise wrote in March 1963,

Now we have had the great joy of welcoming amongst us Dr Agnes Gilruth. Her first week has been a busy one, getting to know the family and helping in the half-yearly medical examinations. Tonight she and Dr Rosemary start off for Kathmandu to get the necessary permit for Dr Gilruth to work in God's Garden. It will be wonderful to have her to carry on the work there when Dr Rosemary has to be away or goes next year on furlough. But doctors need nurses; how crying a need this is.

This prayer, too, was answered in 1964 by the coming of Frances Backhouse to work as a nurse with Agnes Gilruth. Frances had been in India with the Queen Alexandra's Royal Nursing Reserve and had first met Ivy Hill when she was staying as a fellow guest at a Sandes Soldiers Home in Ranikhet in 1947. Years later Ivy Hill and Elise Page linked up again with Frances, then working in Shropshire. They invited her to come back out to work in India. In 1964 Frances felt able to respond to their invitation.

She was encouraged when her letter offering her services arrived a day after Agnes had written to Gorakhpur to say, 'I don't know how much longer I can continue here without help'. The amount of work they got through, as in the Nurseries' dispensaries, was really amazing. In 1969 in God's Garden, 55,000 patients were seen, 71 abnormal maternity cases, 406 minor operations, 362 in-patients cared for. Dr Gilruth writing about her life in God's Garden said,

> The mother of the Headman of the village was ill. He came personally to escort me. The water on the road was over knee deep and then we had to walk up the riverside quite a long way before crossing it at a wide, less deep part. The Headman entered the river first and crossed it without looking back. He was out the other side before I was halfway across.

The mud in his village was as bad as the river, deep and slippery too. Coming back he sent an old man with me who tottered through the river nearer to me but would not have had much strength to help. About two thirds of the way across, I suddenly stepped down into deep water and nearly lost my balance and did not enjoy the experience. Now my nightly prayer is that I may not have to go to the Headman's village again!

She goes on to say that not only from without are there trials at this season.

No foodstuff keeps in this wet atmosphere; the home-made biscuits, fresh last Monday, are already soft, sticky and growing whiskers, though kept in a tin with a tightly fitting lid. When I opened the cupboard I found it crawling with insect life, two tins of sweets a sticky mess, a packet of dried fruit a solid mass. A tin with raisins had worms but Bua has cooked them up tonight and made a sweetmeat and for my sins I have had to eat it, thick with raisins which I do not like anyway, as she had so lovingly prepared it.

The store tin was crawling too, one cake packet was torn and had mites in it – the soup packets looked all right [these would have been sent from home] but I found one leaking and a worm came out, so after we had soaked it and some more came out, we fed it to the hens.

This part of Agnes' letter was headed 'Lay not up for yourselves treasure upon earth, where insects do corrupt!'

In 1975, Maryke van Emmerick had felt called, following the visit of Elise Page and Ivy Hill to the Bible College of Wales where Maryke was training.

She wrote,

> Last year in my first year of the Bible College, Miss
> Page and Miss Hill visited the college and the Lord
> really spoke to my heart through them. Some time
> later, one evening we were praying very much for
> the work of Operation Mobilisation and when I
> went to my room afterwards, I asked the Lord very
> definitely to show me where he wanted me to go
> and what to do. The next morning I found a little
> book, 'God's Garden', on the bookshelf in the dining
> room. As I read it I saw pictures of Miss Page and
> Miss Hill and for me this was the answer of the
> Lord.

So, following correspondence, Maryke arrived to help
Dr Agnes Gilruth and Sister Frances Backhouse in
Nepal.

13

ELISE'S JUBILEE

In 1969, Elise Page celebrated her fifty years at the
Nurseries. Writing about it she says,

> What a joyful day 26th February was, rejoicing from
> beginning to end. Early morning a united
> Communion service for all communicants, later a
> lovely gathering of the whole family, singing and
> 'wishes' and a lovely gift from the Family of a beau-
> tifully worked table cloth (golden colour, of course)
> then more worship and rededication of our lives to
> our Saviour. In the afternoon, sports for all, with
> prizes sent by a lady now living in Assam who was
> baptised in Gorakhpur in 1967.

She goes on: 'Two lovely marks of Jubilee; electricity
throughout the compound for the Family and a new
Frigidaire for us in the bungalow (the old one, thirty
years old, failing to work). Also on our drawing-room
mantelpiece now is a very pretty little clock, a present
from Muriel, Thilde, Matie and Rose, which actually
goes. We had looked at twenty-to-eight for years!'

Looking back on her fifty years, Elise reminisces on
God's goodness to them. She wrote,

> In our Covenant signed by those who join the
> Gorakhpur Nurseries Fellowship is this sentence
> 'God's work, done in God's way, will never lack

God's supplies'. Through the years we have proved this to be abundantly true. 'In God's way' – sometimes, when short of money, we have taken stock and found something had to be put right or something altered. But as we 'seek first the Kingdom of God' (Matthew 6:33), we know all these things shall be added unto us, and they are! Sometimes we are tested. One Christmas, there were enough vests to go round for everyone, only one set of twelve was missing and one bigger one; we just mentioned it to our Heavenly Father. The very next post brought a small parcel and in it were twelve vests, the size we needed and one outsize! Or the day, when the larder was really empty and suddenly news came in the morning, three missionaries will be passing through and will have lunch with us. Within minutes, a thing which has never happened before or since, a complete, lovely English lunch, with all the etceteras, arrived as a gift from someone who had been helped spiritually. Or 'in things great and small', the time I was ill (many years ago) and we were in very low waters and on the human level saw no way through. I said, 'Do you think God has forgotten us?' I could have bitten my tongue out, so faithful has He always been. That very moment the post came – a letter – a legacy of £500, followed two weeks later by another legacy of £500 (donors unknown).

Elise had many beautiful memories too of the family. Writing in 1960, she spoke of the visit of Dr Aqbar Haqq and his family to Gorakhpur to conduct a campaign in a large marquee, capable of holding 2,000. One of the team, who came ahead, visited them and went to the Nurseries revival prayer meeting. Before leaving, the visitor said, 'Thank you for the privilege of being here. I have been blessed and helped. The Presence of the Lord is overwhelming.' Members of the family became counsellors and about twenty helped form the choir.

Elise wrote:

> Then the great opening day came. I must confess to a surge of pride and gratitude to our Heavenly Father for his amazing working in broken lives, to see ours filling a large place in the choir stalls, wrapped in the hand knitted shawls made by our friends – it was cold weather – looking cared for and entirely earnest and eager.
>
> There was an excellent message to appeal to all and at the close, an invitation to anyone who would be glad of help. A number went forward – now was the time for counsellors. We went into the Enquiry Room to help and at least ten of ours were there. My heart leapt for joy and I know how Aunt Molly would be overjoyed to see how now the family can help others to know the Saviour or lead them into a deeper life in God. The cream, perhaps, was when Kamolini [mentioned in Chapter 6] was chosen as Supervisor in the Enquiry Room, to whom all the counsellors and enquirers might turn. She was absolutely in her element, full of the joy of the Lord at this opportunity.

One of the team was introduced to Kamolini's husband. 'Do you realise what a wonderful woman your wife is?' he was asked.

Later, the team came back to visit the Nurseries, partly to thank the family for their gift; their 'tenth' towards the campaign expenses surprised the leaders. One of them said, 'The time has come for us [Indians] to be the pillars of the Church and you,' sweeping his hand towards the family, 'have some here.'

When the Haqqs heard them singing they said, 'It is

like a bit of heaven. This has been the highlight of our visit, we shall never forget it.' It was when the family came through a doorway towards the visitors, in their many-colour 'Sunday saris', one of them said, 'This is too much for me'. Elise agreed, 'Beautiful colours aren't they?' 'Yes, but it is the light on their faces. I've never met anything like it. I wish others could see it too,' the visitor replied.

The family had their own evangelistic weeks each year, and that year, 1960, Elise reported the total number of gospels and tracts sold during the week, by the family, was 4,909 portions, 27 New Testaments and 3 Bibles.

In her Jubilee year, Elise was seventy-eight and she and Matie began to wonder about the future. So, at the end of 1971, after their eightieth birthdays, they announced they were going to retire home to England. It came as a surprise to the other three, Muriel Ainger, Sister Thilde and Rosemary Page. Elise and Matie had for some years spent most of the hot season away from Gorakhpur up in the hills, but they had not actually spoken of going to England for good.

So Muriel, herself aged sixty-nine, took over the leadership of the Fellowship in 1972.

14

MURIEL'S LEADERSHIP –
FRUSTRATIONS BUT PROMISES
FULFILLED

When Muriel became leader, the family numbered one
hundred. They were in two places, the original building
in Gorakhpur, and Jainagar, as they called it, about five
miles outside – this was where Muriel had lived and
worked most of her life in India. They were running
two dispensaries and in 1972, 95,165 patients were
treated. The Buas and older girls made regular trips to
the villages to evangelise and sell books.

In 1972, 450 visits were made, 14,650 Gospels and
Christian books were sold, 124 New Testaments and 25
Bibles.

Considering the size of the family and the amount of
work they were able to do, their running expenses were
remarkable even for 1972. Their receipts were £11,453.
Expenditure on family, Indian and European –
£6,256.18; dispensary and villages – £1,456.89;
Maintenance – £169; vehicle registration, insurance and
licences – £34.86; others – £944.94; transfers – £1,073.25;
making a total of £10,127.58 for all their expenses,
including their own spending money – leaving a balance at the end of the year of £1,325.43. 'Others' included money given to other Christian organisations in
India, Bible Society, Every Home Crusade, Operation
Mobilisation etc.

They had blessings, but there were frustrations also.

In one of her first letters after she took over, Muriel wrote about the problem of renewing the lease for the land that the Nurseries were built on. She said that the land was given to Mary Warburton Booth in the early days by the then Government, in appreciation for her help and services at a time when plague was raging in the city. It was a thirty-year lease which expired in 1967. Elise had started making efforts to get the land lease renewed as early as 1966. Now in 1973, Muriel was still trying to get it settled. She wrote of going to an office and all being sanctioned with only one more signature needed. They thought they would receive the finalised papers. Instead, they were informed that there was a 'defect in wording' and the leases would have to be redrafted. As they were drawn up by the lawyer appointed by the Government it was difficult to understand.

It was not until June 1975 that Muriel was able to write, 'Yesterday the main part of the Gorakhpur leases was signed and registered – so – let us praise His Name together. For eight years you have prayed and we have wrestled. If we added up the hours spent over the business it would come to months of working hours.'

Although they were recognised as a charitable institution, and therefore exempt from income tax, there were many formalities which had to be meticulously observed and audited by chartered accountants, and all the income tax returns to be filled in.

Muriel wrote, 'There is endless paper work.' She went on,

> One of the wearing things about life out here is that it is rarely possible to get a thing 'ticked off'. Our Fellowship Registration seemed to be completed satisfactorily, with only the routine information to be sent each year and the re-application for registration every two years. Some weeks ago we received a long

document from the Registrar demanding still further from us – what? We now have to ask one of our Indian friends to go himself to the Registrar's office in Lucknow and find out for us exactly what it is they want.

He did this, taking copies of all their recent correspondence. It was agreed that all that was necessary had been done and when asked why the constant demands for papers that had already been received, the amazing reply was – 'Well we must have something to do in the office'.

Now that Elise and Matie had retired, Muriel realised that it was not possible to go on manning the work in two places as they had been doing. So, in November 1973, she wrote to prayer partners about the great change that was to take place. She described it as the biggest thing they had had to face since the work first began. 'We are sure,' she wrote, 'that it is the Lord's time for us to move the family from Gorakhpur to Jainagar.' It was not a new thought, a sudden decision. In fact in the 1930s, when she was acquiring land, Mary Warburton Booth had said of Jainagar that 'one day this will be the place where the family lives'.

In Gorakhpur, the wide open spaces that surrounded their property were increasingly being encroached upon, so that now they were completely encircled and blocked in. On one side they were overlooked by two-storey buildings, while shops were being built on either side of their front gate, bringing previously unheard-of crowds to them. The noise was incessant day and night. Increasingly it was not a good or safe environment to bring up a family of girls.

Jainagar was five miles outside the city and still in comparative countryside. Also they had plenty of land there on which to build and expand. So, after much prayer and thought, it was decided that all the family should be together there. There were various pointers to the fact that this might be the right time. For one thing, in a wonderful way through one of their Trustees, a building supervisor, Vijay Charan, known as Bobby, was appointed.

So the building began. The amazing sustaining, guiding and undertaking for them at this period could be a book in itself. Reading Muriel's letters at this time it doesn't take much imagination to realise the pressures and yet the amazing sense of God being in control, under which Muriel, Thilde and Rose lived in those days. Writing in September 1974, Muriel said, 'We are still in the process of moving. The end of June found the main buildings well up but a tremendous amount of detail and various extensions remained to be finished.'

Then came the heavy monsoon, the worst floods for many years in Gorakhpur. Although they escaped the more severe, they were constantly under water – there were even fish in the compound. Work was very much slowed down. So they were in two places and at times, Muriel said, rather confused as to which end things were at.

In July, she wrote, 'Our Building Supervisor moved on to his next job so that we have had the overseeing of the remaining details', and she rather characteristically adds, 'a full-time job though intensely interesting'.

I remember going around the site with her when she was building supervisor and she pointed to a building in construction, right in the centre of one side of the compound. They had built hostels, babies nursery, houses for the Buas who cared for them, office block and school rooms, and the building which Muriel was indicating was meant to be a kindergarten. However, for some reason which even he himself could not explain, the builder had gone on building the walls much higher than was needed for a kindergarten.

Muriel said that when she saw it, she suddenly realised that it was not a mistake, but right; it was a much better place than the one they had planned for their Praise Hall. So the change was made and they had, as it should be, their centre of worship at the nub of the compound.

In age-conscious Britain, no one would put a woman of over seventy, even one with a lot of wisdom, in charge of building supervision. She was of course also 'mother' to a family of over one hundred. Unlike the West, in the East the older you are the more respect you receive, and to God, who sent Moses when he was over seventy to lead the children of Israel into the promised land, age is often not the most relevant matter. It's the person for the job and not the age he looks at. The move itself, from one building to the next, had also, in a sense, to be Master-minded.

Muriel wrote:

The great move is on.

November 13th, 1974:
The Bethany babies moved into Bethlehem, their new home, with a name more suited to the very young. This move took quite a bit of arranging. Previously the houses had been cleaned and prepared and some furniture brought in. On the day, each baby and toddler had to be provided with a pair of arms and a lap for maximum comfort in the car. The tiny babies came out in the first car load, after their morning feeds, with Kamila [one of the Buas] and Sister Thilde. The slightly older came later with Rose Page, each one with her personal attendant. All sizes of babies were then in Jainagar for their rest and meal. [Muriel was in Jainagar to receive them all.] Each party was welcomed with a banner and songs.

18th November:
The rest of the family arrived from Gorakhpur to
live in the new family house, Bethany. The Buas had
been out to get their own rooms ready, the children
were spick and span as if for a party, the Buas happy
and undaunted by the mountains of luggage that
kept arriving.

There were no removal vans. They had thought at first
to use a truck but decided that they could not cope with
the loading and unloading. So they used a local trans-
porter of goods called a Thela. This is a contraption of
planks rather like a long raft, eight to ten feet long and
about three feet wide, balanced on two wheels and
pushed and pulled by four men. The secret of loading is
the balance. Muriel said, 'We watched with admiration
as our good team of men loaded up our motley collec-
tion of cupboards, bins, iron beds, school chairs and
desks, boxes, family furniture, contents of family
kitchens and store houses and then tucked into available spaces, bundles, baskets, bird cages etc.'
Sister Thilde stayed the night of the 18th in
Gorakhpur. On 19th November the family was complete – they were all safely at Jainagar. The leading
verse in *Daily Light* that night was, 'I will make the
place of My feet glorious' – the same promise that was
given in the beginning for Jainagar thirty-eight years
before. That was to them a gracious confirmation of the
Lord's leading.
Back at the old Nurseries building in Gorakhpur, an
Indian pastor had come to live and he called a team
from the Allahabad Bible Seminary to be with him.
They visited the area and then had meetings in the compound for any especially interested. Later, it was a particular joy when Operation Mobilisation (OM), an
organisation who are motivated to use young people in
evangelisation, moved into the compound. They used it

as a centre for training and evangelism in the city and surrounding district, a dream the Nurseries folk had had for many years.

15

NEW BUILDINGS

Muriel was so glad to have everyone together in Jainagar. Next year, 1975, their special chorus was:

> Come walk with me round the walls of the city
>   See what the King has been building so well.
> Put down your tools, rest awhile from your labours,
>   Lift up your eyes, lift up your hands, come and see.
> Come dance with me round the walls of the city,
>   Let us give glory to Jesus our King.

'We are still thinking,' she wrote, 'in terms of building and its spiritual lessons, our Foundation Jesus Christ, also our Cornerstone, we the bricks in the building. But separate bricks, however good, never make a house; it needs the joining in love, in unity, then we can make a worthy dwelling for "Jesus our King".'

There was still work to do to complete the buildings and roofs, and brick paths to be laid after the ground had settled. They had workmen in to do these jobs and Dr Rose Page oversaw this work, going round the compound on a cycle. 'A great incentive to diligence,' Muriel wrote, 'as the workmen never know from which direction she will suddenly appear.' Rose, a medical doctor, as with the others, was ready to do any job that was needed. Versatility, not specialisation, was the order of the day. They had a very good team of Indians who came in to work on the land and building. They did the manual work, but the ladies did the direction and supervising.

The responsibility for the care of the property fell to Muriel in Jainagar. Every year there was a hot weather and cold weather schedule. In the heat, chairs were moved under the fan, carpets taken up, rugs, cushions, anything that might make it feel cooler. Then in September/October came the annual whitewashing and the changing back to the winter routine.

It is interesting how many people in Britain seem to think that because you worked in India or Nepal you must like the climate. Muriel found the heat very difficult and in May and June it could be over 110 degrees. In a heat wave in England she would find it quite trying, to say the least, to have people say to her, 'I suppose this is how you like the weather'. In fact she was never happier than in December and January when they could sit round a log fire in the sitting room in the cool evenings. She was always sad when it became too hot to do so.

One of Muriel's great loves was gardening and she made the grounds of Jainagar really beautiful. She planned the new look of Jainagar and in the monsoon planted trees. She wrote in November 1975,

> The trees are growing well, and the grass is coming up so that the new part of the compound begins to look really established. It is a busy time on the land, winter crops such as wheat, gram and peas are being sown and we are greatly extending our vegetable garden, as vegetables are so expensive. These, curried, are the family's main food. Flowers too are not forgotten; the family love their flower patches and the little ones enjoy watering, including themselves, most liberally.

'Also this year,' she went on, 'the monsoon has been excessive and went on very late. Only those who have lived through a long monsoon will know the toll on body, mind and spirit. Because of the monsoon, white-washing and spring cleaning had to be delayed.'

Muriel also supervised the land and the planting of crops that helped to make them self-sufficient. Writing about it one March:

> Today in Jainagar our wheat is being harvested, cut by hand with the sickle as in Bible days. Our land has been greatly blessed. We have had abundant supplies of fruit and vegetables, a very good rice harvest in September and now a specially bonny crop of wheat. This really is the goodness of God as a few miles north of us the crops were decimated by hail storms. A tremendous help to us is a power tiller – mini tractor, a gift to us, known now as Tilly – she greatly increases production. In these days of general shortness, we are trying to cultivate every available bit of ground.

Muriel comments that she broke off writing here to go to get Tilly started off on the threshing floor. She then continues, 'She is now doing a good job by going round in circles on the bundles of wheat. Such a relief to see her fat wheels rotating instead of the slow tread of oxen hooves.'

16

THE FAMILY AND NEW MEMBERS

When Muriel first went to Jainagar, she had with her Sitaria, a little seven-year-old girl. Sitaria stayed on and became the Bua in charge of all the family at Jainagar. Naulini, the Bua in charge in Gorakhpur, had been one of the first seven children Aunt Molly took in. She was now old and frail and was glad for Sitaria to take charge of the whole family. Sitaria, a quiet, dignified person, was rather nervous as she faced her new responsibilities. She said, 'The family has been small and will now be big. I thought how can I cope when they are all here from Gorakhpur? But I prayed and the Lord said "My grace is sufficient for you" – and it is so true.'

Muriel wrote,

Sitaria was really brimming over with pleasure as she said, 'This year the Lord so specially blessed our Christmas feast. There was enough for the evening meal too and again the next day a little left to be eaten with chapatis. Praise the Lord.'

Christmas is always a busy time. First those away in their own homes are remembered with greetings, Bible reading cards and a monthly magazine being sent to all 140 of them, these days. Then to those with families we send a parcel of clothing and warm things plus smaller joys. Every parcel has to be sewn up and sealed for safety. After the parcels are sent away, we can start our preparations for the family Christmas, everyone receiving a present.

Every 23rd December is a Thanksgiving Day. In 1975 this was held in the new Praise Hall, with its colourful blue paint, flowers and poinsettia decorations and dedication banners. The many-coloured garments of the family who were all tightly packed and sitting on the floor, made a gay carpet. For practical reasons the dedication of the babies comes first.

Muriel wrote,

> There is a line of babies, each warmly clad in woollies [it is cold in Gorakhpur in December], bonnets, bootees, shawls and held lovingly in the arms of the Buas, all standing in the front. Each baby brought during the year is, by name, put into the hands of the Lord Jesus, our Christmas present to Him. We pray for them that they will grow up to be true followers of the Lord Jesus. That year there were three babies, whose names – translated to English – mean Music, Melody and Praise [Muriel commented, 'we hope that will come true'], also, a tiny boy Beautiful Prince [again Muriel commented, 'what a lot to live up to' Hindu names all have meaning].

The baby boys had to be adopted. They had not felt it right to start a separate home for boys. Experience in other places had shown that it led to all sorts of complications if unrelated boys and girls grew up together in a segregated community. In Dohnavur in South India, the work most like the Nurseries, Amy Carmichael had men called to the fellowship, and so she kept the boys sent to the family. The work is now run by Indians and only takes girls, the boys being adopted, the pattern the Nurseries had felt was right for them from the beginning.

In 1975, there were four boys for whom they were seeking adoptive parents – a great responsibility. Recently they had had a very happy adoption of a lovely baby boy. The parents had lost two of their own children and the mother was longing for this little one and she wrote so gratefully after they reached home 'with our little son'.

Arranging weddings too was always a matter of prayer and concern.

'Around this time,' Muriel wrote,

there have been some happy visits from our married Indrabai and her husband from Mauritius. It was a really romantic story of a young Indian man who came from Mauritius in search of a bride, and after much travelling and many vicissitudes, found her at the Nurseries. He became the Principal of a large College in Mauritius and they took a leading part in Christian activities there. Another from Bareilly in India came, and then one married to a Nepali and working there.

In a country where arranged marriages are the norm, Muriel and the others had to take responsibility for those wishing to be married. It is very wonderful, over the years, how in answer to prayer God provided husbands for the girls. They received many invitations to the weddings of 'their' girls. Perhaps the prize one was:

In the moving wheel of life 15th October 1986 is an auspicious day when Mr. and Mrs. Walter Singh feel pleasure to chain up their son D.K. Walter in wedlock with Harshit Singh. Your gracious presence is solicitated.

It was to be a happy 'locking together'!

Muriel, writing in a letter in 1977, spoke of one of their teachers who had gone with others to Allahabad to attend Spiritual Life meetings. While there, a young ex-student of the Bible Seminary saw her and, though they had no other contact, it seems to have been love at first sight. He then put things in motion and asked a friend to contact the Nurseries and ask for her in marriage, even suggesting the wedding date! Muriel protested and said that wouldn't do, they hadn't even met and talked with each other. The reply came back, 'It is not necessary, I want her and no other.' He had quite failed to see that the girl also had a say in the matter! When they insisted that he took the long journey from his home, he appeared very suitable to them and to the girl! There was a happy engagement, and wedding in July and the couple went to work together in a mining area where there was a group of Christians. She helped with house meetings and Sunday School. Later that year, another just-right wedding was arranged; a keen young man, a Christian who had his own dry cleaning business and was the friend of a pastor, the husband of one of the Nurseries girls. It is nice when several Nursery girls are married in the same area; they can keep together as real sisters.

Muriel, in the same letter, wrote of the difficulties some of their family were facing. One had recently lost her husband, another had a husband who had developed a serious heart condition and another herself was seriously ill. There are, Muriel reminded her readers, no social services and there is often discrimination against Christians. 'We pray constantly that our Family away will remain true and faithful, remembering all they learnt while with us.'

Although there had been changes both in society and in the location of the Nurseries, there was no doubt they were still needed. Writing in 1978 of recent arrivals, Muriel spoke of Anita and Punita, who had been abandoned as toddlers in a hospital in western India. The hospital officials tried to trace the parents while the toddlers just ran wild. As they could not stay on, when no parents were found, a friend of the

Nurseries arranged for them to go there – they were a real handful at first!

Another, Champa, born illegitimately, had been abandoned and would have died had the Nurseries not taken her when she was one month old. Jaiwanti came just a day old, having been born to a very young mother who could not keep her. Shirola, six months old, was found in a field and taken to a nearby mission hospital and sent from there to the Nurseries. Shunila was born of a mother mentally afflicted and would have been cast out. Then one day, Bishwasi Bua from God's Garden arrived unexpectedly, carrying a carton in which a small baby girl was warmly tucked up. The mother had died in a village near the dispensary and the father had no relatives and no means of caring for the baby.

Another had come when they had gone on an expedition towards the Nepal border, to sell gospels to crowds coming back from a big mela in Nepal. They dropped one party off at a strategic place and went on to the border to meet someone from God's Garden to hand over supplies. There was an interchange and an eighteen-month-old girl was brought and handed over. The mother had died and the child was very undernourished, with a thin neck, large head and very sombre eyes. Muriel, writing about her, said,

> She is very self-possessed and gave no trouble on the motor journey back. All she wanted was food and greeted everything with a round mouth 'oh'. She settled in at once and the other day we saw her, being taken along by another 'small', two sizes taller, who was taking her hand and bending solicitously over her. A new baby is the greatest family excitement. 'A new baby has come' is the cry and from all corners of the compound children pour out to see their little sister.

Many of the children who come to the Nurseries come from Mission Hospitals. Baby girls, even today, are simply abandoned when the mother discovers she has a girl. They are left in the hospital compounds, knowing the Christians will find them and take care of them.

For example, when Shashi was found she had her right hand terribly burnt. It is not known what happened to her, but with open fires in the middle of mud floors, it is not unusual, in the night when the family is asleep on mats around the fire, for a baby to roll into it. A baby girl, with an injured hand, would not be a good marriageable proposition, so better to get rid of her by leaving her to be found near the Mission Hospital. Shashi's right hand is permanently clenched like a fist, and has just (in 1997) had plastic surgery on her good left hand as, with growth, burns contractions were beginning to flex her fingers on that hand too.

Vandana was left alone in the compound of Raxaul Hospital, Bihar, North India. She had extensive leucoderma (big white areas on body, limbs and forehead). Again, she was probably abandoned because her parents thought they would never get her married. She is now twelve and in 1997 was baptised at her own request.

Another baby, Swaran, was found by a woman suffering from leprosy when she was picking up pieces of coal on the railway line. She saw a bit of rag move; on investigation she found that the bundle of rags contained a baby girl, so the woman took the baby to the railway police. 'We don't want it,' they said. 'Take it to the mission!' So newborn Swaran came to the Nurseries. She thrived and was able to go to school. She grew up and later married a Christian electrician and they now have a baby daughter.

Uma was brought to the Nurseries within hours of her birth. Her young unmarried mother was brought to Gorakhpur by her own mother who made arrangements for her daughter's confinement at a private nursing home. The Nurseries never saw either mother or grandmother, the baby was brought by one of the staff, not long after her birth. If the Nurseries had not been there, Uma would not have survived. Kamla, the Bua in charge, was delighted to have a new baby which had not had time to get a tummy upset or any infection. Uma has grown up well and is now at school doing her A levels.

Later Kirti and Kiran came, within a month of each other, from the same private clinic. The Nurseries gathered that had they not been brought to them they would have been put in the dustbin! Sadly female infanticide is still widely practised. Kirti and Kiran are now seven years old and go to the local primary school.

Working in Nepal I, too, was very glad the Nurseries were there. A Brahmin (high caste) man with tuberculosis came bringing a very small scrap of a little girl. He said his wife had died having her, he himself was dying of tuberculosis and had no one to look after his baby. Please would I take her as he knew then she would be cared for. At first I felt that he should be helped to keep her and so I supplied milk and other needs. Then a Nepali friend said, 'Mary, please take her, then he can die happy, knowing that his daughter will be well cared for.' So eventually I took her, and shortly after she became part of the Nurseries family, her father died. She has recently been happily married.

Another two delightful children, a boy and a girl, were abandoned in the hospital in Tansen. We tried in vain to trace their parents and they too joined the Gorakhpur family. They were inseparable and were adopted, with great success, by a childless couple known to the Nurseries.

The greatest joy at the Nurseries was when those who came as babies, asked for baptism and then showed fruits of their decision in their lives. Muriel in one of her letters said that, as she was preparing to write, ten girls between twelve and fifteen years of age, with shining faces, came into her room. 'Please, we want to be baptised. The Lord has spoken to us,' they said. Lotus, mentioned in Mary Warburton Booth's books, had taken meetings during the hot weather with them and this was their response. They had found assurance of salvation. There was no doubt about their sincerity. Muriel said no one was just baptised after asking. There was always preparation, individual talks and also classes, for this is a really serious step and they did not want them to feel it could be taken lightly. She wrote, 'Such events are truly our overweights of joy'.

Stories like these go on until the present day (1997). The need for abandoned children to be cared for and loved remains. Thank God the Nurseries are still there to meet this need.

17

ADDITIONS, CELEBRATION, LOSSES, CHANGES

The pressure of the work on Sister Thilde, Muriel and Rosemary was great, so they were very glad when in 1981 Irene Rudling joined them.

Muriel wrote about it in November 1981:

We have specially joyful news to give you. A very dear friend of ours and of the family's is joining us in the life and work here. Irene Rudling has been in India for twelve years in a Christian school, Wynberg Allen, in Mussoorie in the mountains of North India, first as a PE Teacher, latterly as Hostel Supervisor in the Junior School, while still keeping on her games coaching. These hill schools, due to the intense cold, have their long holiday in the winter and Irene has spent most of her holidays with us, joining in all our activities. She can turn her hand to anything, from helping to dress babies for the Thanksgiving Service to making a cushion cover for the sitting room. Life here is full of variety, sometimes rather too full. The possibility of Irene joining us has been in our hearts and minds for some time, but it was not clear as to how and when. Now the Lord has made a 'plain path' for her to come. Her contract with the school comes to an end this month. She will bring all her luggage during the last week of November, stay for a week then take her normal three months leave in England. At the end of

February (DV) she will return to us 'for keeps'.
What a blessed prospect and how we look forward
to this. Two weeks ago, after Sunday Service, I told
the Family to their huge delight and asked the Buas
'Had you ever thought of such a happy thing?' 'Oh
yes,' they said, 'we've been praying for this very
thing for a long time.'

The day after Muriel told the family, one of the kindergarten children asked 'Has Miss Lodling come yet?!' It
was easier when she came and was given the family
name, Siti Ji (mother's sister).

Irene's coming was particularly joyous for Muriel as
she had known her since the early 1960s when they had
met at a meeting Muriel took in Eastbourne. Friends of
Irene's, Alex and Muriel Johnson, had been prayer supporters of the Nurseries for years and had invited Irene
to the meeting. Then began a long train of events which
ended in her becoming part of the family.

It is interesting that Irene too, like Thilde and
Muriel, had applied to Dohnavur and been told that
they had no need of anyone with her qualifications at
that time. What a loss for the Nurseries if they had all
been accepted by Dohnavur! We need to remember in
life that the doors God shuts as well as the ones he
opens are in his plans for our lives.

Irene quickly settled into the work; she, of course,
knew a lot about it already.

Muriel writing in November 1982 says, 'Siti Ji (I.R.)
is now settled in Elim [one of their houses] as if she had
always been with us and is getting on well with the language. She takes the younger ones' Bible lesson, teach-
es English in two of the school classes, is beginning to
take over the care of the children's clothes, a very big
job, organises games in the evenings and much else.'

In the changing society of India, and the need for
education for all their girls, the Nurseries folk needed to

keep in touch with what was going on. Irene took over the school affairs, and she visited colleges and schools, making suggestions and changes where these were considered necessary for the progress of the girls.

Irene was pleased to be at the Nurseries for Muriel's eightieth birthday, and writing about it, she said:

> Muriel didn't celebrate the 50th anniversary of her coming but decided her 80th birthday should be special. Plans laid beforehand included a shopping expedition to buy a present for each one in the family, from the youngest to the oldest. The list was long; so many pencil boxes, stainless steel plates etc. etc . . . wonderfully we were able to get the right number of each item and came home triumphant. As usual [everyone who is at the Nurseries on their birthday is greeted in this way] all the family gathered at 6 a.m. to sing Happy Birthday and offer their present. It was a lovely, specially chosen, sari for Muriel.

After breakfast they gathered together on Jerusalem, the big verandah in front of the office. With great joy and surprise everyone received a present and then, age group by age group, sang a chorus or a hymn. Muriel shared something of the way the Lord had led her all through these years, and of his faithfulness, and she concluded with prayer.

Meanwhile in secret, Irene, Rose and Thilde had been trying to get a 'dream' of Muriel's and give it to her as a surprise present. For several years she had voiced the wish for a tricycle, to get about the large compound, especially when overseeing the garden work. 'I don't want a saddle,' she had said, 'but a comfortable seat in which to sit and oversee the sowing of seeds or planting out of vegetables.'

Rosemary, inspired by an invalid carriage she had

seen, planned together with a local worker in iron goods and produced a marvellous vehicle in time for the great day – later to be named Trixie. The ironworker entered into the spirit of the surprise and made sure he brought the finished item the day before the birthday, via the back gate, so it could be hidden overnight.

When Muriel came for elevenses, there stood Trixie on the path outside the sitting-room door. She was in it at once and had to have a trial run all round the family compound, an admiring crowd of children following excitedly behind.

In the afternoon she took her usual siesta, but after tea there was a lively Sports Day, all the children taking part in three or four events each and, as a finale, there was a Buas' obstacle race. Even now all was not over! They had a special supper all together, sitting in a big circle outdoors and, as the light gradually faded, the Buas let off a few fireworks, sending up showers of tiny stars into the sky – a beautiful end to a memorable day.

In March 1987, Muriel wrote:

The great excitement of January was a visit to Bombay. Three of the Buas, two for the second time, one for the first, went with Siti Ji (Irene) on their memorable adventure. We have friends in Bombay who belong to a living, growing church, the New Life Fellowship. They arranged a splendid programme whereby our group shared in the life of the Fellowship and their many activities. This is something our girls have never experienced and they returned full of enthusiasm and with a new vision of what the Lord is doing through the people in the country. There was also ample time for sightseeing. The aquarium and the airport were visited and there was a trip by boat to famous caves. Next the great joy was paddling and collecting shells. None in our family had ever seen the sea. It was altogether a very well worthwhile time and enlarging in every way, made possible by a special gift for something outside the normal routine.

Talking of gifts, the work of the Nurseries has always been controlled and guided by the people in India. There are no home committees making decisions about money or personnel. No one receives a salary. From the beginning, however, friends and family have been a strong support for the Nurseries Fellowship. The Hon Margaret Strutt, a friend of Aunt Molly's, first took responsibility for channelling any funds which came in for them out to India. Then Mrs Kitty Clouston, Rosemary's cousin, took over from Miss Strutt in 1971. She continued to do it until she died in 1989. Miss Denise Earthy then took over and is continuing to do so up to the time of writing.

Aunt Molly felt that the work should be backed by prayer, so she sent out regular newsletters three times a year. This custom has continued and they are distributed by friends, at their own expense, to prayer partners all over the country. Prayer has been a real power house for the work down the years.

In 1958, Muriel and the others were surprised to receive a large doll for the family from a single man named Tony Devis. It appears he had heard of the work through Down Lodge Hall in Wandsworth where he lived and had felt he should send the doll. As the years passed, his links with the Fellowship deepened and he became a very great support for the work. When he died in 1979 Muriel wrote, 'Tony was indeed God's good gift to us, to the Fellowship and to the family. He had not visited us here but his understanding and discernment were remarkable, Spirit given.' From 1958, as long as there was a Christian Holiday camp at Filey, Tony ran a stall for the Gorakhpur Nurseries. He was always whole-heartedly in the work. He looked after the books and leaflets relating to the Nurseries and sent out slides, gave information etc. and he was also responsible for sending out the newsletter to friends in the north of England. After his marriage, his wife Joy also fully shared his interest and loving concern for the Fellowship. She too felt knit into the work and valued so much Muriel's letters, support and friendship. Over the years Muriel's letters were the sort that people kept, to give comfort and encouragement, and this Joy did. After Tony's death she felt she should take over the work that he had been doing.

Muriel and the others appreciated very much the prayer and support given by those at home. Writing in 1986 Muriel said,

Always as I begin these letters there is a warm feeling of encouragement, knowing that our news goes to you who love and care for the family and all that goes on here. How often when things have been particularly difficult and contrary have we been conscious of your prayer upholding and been strengthened to go on. Sometimes a way has suddenly opened where there had been uncertainties, or new light has come on a complicated situation, and we have known that some have been praying and sharing with us in spirit.

18

A DAY IN MURIEL'S LIFE

Muriel, although in her eighties, continued to have very busy, disciplined days. Irene Rudling writing about it says,

'She would most likely be woken by the dawn chorus, numerous birds singing their welcome to a new day, the drongo, a small black bird with a forked tail, the dayal or Indian robin, perhaps the lovely notes of the golden oriole and the tiresome tonk tonk of the coppersmith. As they sang, she would enjoy a banana and a cup of tea or two from the flask at her bedside.

'Before getting involved in the work of the day, her first joy would be to meet with the Lord as she read the Word and prayed. Besides her King James version she always used several other translations and explored the deeper meaning of words, using the Amplified Bible which she very much appreciated. She was always very meticulous and kept careful notes of anything special the Lord revealed to her, not I think daily, but from time to time. She was never one to get in a rut!

'In winter the men who worked in the garden and fields reported for duty to her at 7 a.m., and in summer at 6 a.m. By then she must be dressed in her sari and ready to receive the milk, which two of the men who kept buffaloes brought for both family and cottage, and to give them instructions for work for the day.

'The family have their breakfast early and soon after, several of the older girls would arrive at the cottage with cheerful 'good mornings' as they set to, to sweep and dust the rooms. Although the family speak Hindi, there are certain phrases they use in English – 'good morning' being one of them. At this time Muriel would probably have a few things to do in the kitchen, in preparation for our breakfast – measuring out tea leaves, setting out eggs (from our own chickens) with a particular sign to Pushpa to indicate how they were to be cooked – e.g. sitting them in an egg cup if to be boiled, or in a basin with a fork beside them if scrambled was the choice for the day.

'Still not breakfast time though. At 7.30 a.m. in winter and 7 a.m. in summer, the bell would ring, summoning everyone to 'Prayers'. The family divide into three groups – classes Kindergarten to III, IV to VI and the older girls and Buas (girls in classes 8–12 would be away in boarding school). This is a main teaching time lasting half an hour. An excellent course, going right through the books of the Bible, with attractive flannel-graphs to help, is used for the girls and the older ones would have a Bible Study series on a particular theme, doctrine or set book of the Bible.

'All the missionaries take turns leading the different age groups. As a teacher, Muriel was excellent with the young ones, making the stories live and applying the truths in a practical way. Her love for the Word and her Saviour shone through her teaching, and the Buas and older girls were always pleased when it was Muriel's turn with them.

'At last the bell would ring for our breakfast and, except in the very coldest months of December and January, we sit at the table outside to enjoy our eggs followed by chapatis and marmalade – the latter home-made.

'Another of Muriel's skills was her housekeeping ability and she saw our larder was kept full of good things – within the range of what was available in this country. Latterly she did not do so much herself but both Sitaria Bua and Pushpa learnt jam making, as well as bottling and preserving, from her. Thus in the very hot summer months, when little is available in the way of fresh vegetables, we could enjoy carrots, turnips and occasionally peas with our meals (sadly the latter did not always 'take' as the bottles failed to seal properly).

'Breakfast over, Muriel would discuss the day's menus with Pushpa and then take a turn round the garden, walking stick in hand and her dog at her heels. 'Was the soil in the seed beds sufficiently fine, did the roses need spraying, or the vegetables need weeding? How far back should the bougainvillaea be trimmed, were the tomatoes ready for picking, if so they must be gathered before the crows got them. Which was the next area where the grass should be cut? The five or six men, many with us since boyhood, work quite well, but need constant supervision and direction.

'Now though, office work would be pressing, letters concerning 101 details, to do with our girls' education or futures, to be written. Trustees to be informed on some matter, married girls with problems wanting advice or help, the variety was legion. Maybe there would be accounts to be checked, money to be given, to Bari Bua for family food, plans to be made for a Bua's holiday or girls to be fetched from boarding school for the summer break. Is the weather hotting up? Then do we have sufficient material for the toddlers' sunsuits, girls needing new school blouses? They must be measured and the material put ready for the darzi (tailor) when he comes. September and the weather will be cool in the early mornings before long, do we need to buy in wool to knit sweaters? Each season brought its needs and life was full and varied, with never any time to become bored.

'Perhaps the coffers were getting low and a visit to Gorakhpur was necessary, to go to the Bank or maybe do some shopping. Bank work was always what Muriel called 'patience producing'. Inevitably one of the men in the chain of those needed to do the work before one could receive money in the hand would be missing. He'd gone to drink tea! 'Please sit and wait a few minutes' would be the request . . . and a few minutes would become 10–15–20!

'Somewhere in the busy days, time must be found to prepare the lesson for the next day's prayers, no easy task, when it has to be done in Hindi.

'Lunch was usually at 12 midday, though advanced to 12.30 if one had been out to town. Most days it would be Indian food – rice and lentils, or a curry, followed by fruit, of which in season there is an abundance in this country – oranges, bananas, mangoes, lychees, grapes, melons, papaya – the list is endless. Pushpa can also make a good stew, though from buffalo meat, and once a month we enjoy a joint of roast pork. One of Aunt Molly's maxims was that for a missionary to work well she must eat well, and sleep well and Muriel certainly saw this was carried on. After lunch we would pray together – praising the Lord for help given and laying before Him needs for that day or problems that needed an answer.

'In true Indian style, lunch was followed by a siesta and Muriel retired thankfully to bed to read or to snooze until teatime, usually 3.30 although variable. In the cooler winter months this too is enjoyed outdoors on the verandah, looking across to the flower border, bright with colour and the gracious eucalyptus trees round our border. In the longer hot season, tea must be taken indoors, sitting in a circle under the fan. Usually the day's post would reach us just before tea and letters would be shared at this time.

'Often the letters would bring matters to be dealt with and more office work. The men's work must be checked and decisions made for the next day, sometimes things to be done that needed Muriel's oversight – vegetable seeds to be sown, chrysanthemum cuttings to be taken etc.

'If it was Monday, then the first hour after tea would be taken up with Mending. Buas would come to her with needs for their children's clothes – elastic, buttons or press studs. Maybe some child had outgrown her school tunic or worn the seat bare by constantly sliding down the shute, and these must be replaced from the second-hand store. If it were Thursday then she would be meeting together with the Buas in the quietness of Peace Cottage sitting room for a time of fellowship and prayer – the 'power house' of our lives together she used to call it.

'Work continued for Muriel at least until 6 p.m. then she would usually bath and change into a housecoat and maybe relax a little with the newspaper or one of the regular periodicals she subscribed to in order to keep in touch with the wider world. We would have a light supper at 7 p.m. again, under the fan in the summer, but in winter (November to February) there was the special joy of sitting by a blazing log fire. Another of Aunt Molly's practices was 'no work after supper', so we would relax together, read, listen to music, do some mending or most often enjoy a game of Scrabble . . . until approximately 8.30 p.m. and time for prayers and bed! Very early you may exclaim . . . and indeed it was for any visitors, especially if with us from overseas . . . but not for Muriel, whose day had begun at 5 a.m. or earlier.'

19

BUAS AND MARRIAGES

One of the lovely things about the Nurseries is how many of the children, as they grow, feel called to stay and care for other children in 'families', just as they themselves had been looked after.

Muriel's right-hand helper in Jainagar was Sitaria who moved out with her when she first went there. Sitaria was then seven and a half years old. She became a trusted and reliable colleague, and as I write now in 1997, is in charge of supervising and looking after the supplies and needs of all the family. They are divided into groups, each with a Bua who becomes mother to her family, but Sitaria has the overall supervision.

Muriel, writing in 1981 about counting their blessings at Christmas said,

This year those who are responsible for a certain area in the life here gave a testimony. Sitaria, the Bua in charge of the family and all the food arrangements, told how each month, in spite of rising prices, there has always been enough money for all needs 'never once have we been short'. I found myself thinking of the person as much as her words. Sitaria was here before I was, in the first kindergarten and as a three year old, one of the moodiest and most unpleasant children I have ever had to deal with. She must have been quite a child for Muriel, with all her experience, to say that!] Truly, I looked at her and thought – what a wonderful work of the Lord, in this serene, capable woman, wholly the Lord's, and our trusted co-worker. She has a heavy responsibility.

Sitaria, writing about Muriel (Phuphu Ji) after she had died said,

I remember that when Phuphu Ji first came, at that time I was three or four years old, she became my teacher in school. We were seven girls and Naulini Bua also taught us. Then after Mama Ji [Aunt Molly] bought this place, Jainagar, she put us seven girls here with Phuphu Ji and Bahin Ji [Thilde]. We were twelve years old. In 1938 we had seven little children, like Sharola, with us here. From that time especially, Phuphu Ji taught me and gave me good training. About six years later Nibha and Shobha and their group joined us and Phuphu Ji trained them too. When any child was ill, Phuphu Ji would come and sit on her bed and talk to her so lovingly. [In view of her dislike of illness, this was rather wonderful.] So the children were happy. For her holidays she went with Mama Ji to Kashmir, because we children were so naughty. [I think they needed a break from the heat as much as the pressures of the work. But an interesting perspective on their holidays from a child's point of view.] I was the naughtiest! She always prayed for us. One time when she was away, all seven of us girls received the Holy Spirit. From that time there was a change in our lives. When she came back from her holiday we told her, with great joy. She said 'Thik hai' [that is right, or good].

Although thrilled and delighted at any new spiritual experience anyone had, Muriel was never over the top about it, keeping her strong spiritual perceptions based, one felt, in realism.

Sitaria wrote,

> Then I remember that she used to take the 8th class
> for drawing. She taught very well, going round the
> class to each girl's desk and saying 'Look, this is the
> way to do it'. She was perfect in the drawing instruc-
> tion she gave us, that's why so many of us began to
> draw well. Whenever she saw me looking sad, she
> would come and tell me something funny to cheer
> me up. I can never forget her love. I still remember
> her love and whenever I go to Zion Cottage, I imag-
> ine her coming out of her room to talk to me. All the
> time she was here, I worked with her and in that
> way I got thoroughly trained, so that I can now look
> after the Family. She used to lead us also in the
> Prayer Meetings and always taught us and helped
> us to grow spiritually.
>
>   So I thank the Lord very, very, very much for her
> life.

For forty years, a very special person in the family was
Kamla. She was Anglo Indian and came to the
Nurseries as a baby. She felt that she had a special call
to look after the babies who came and was never really
happy unless she had a small baby in her care. She was
regularly praying for new babies to come to the
Nurseries, as the ones she was looking after started to
grow up. God answered her prayers and kept her well
supplied!

One such answer was in July 1973. Muriel wrote in
her regular letter home to Prayer Partners,

> This time I must begin with our really exciting news.
> We've got triplets!! eight days old, three tiny Nepali
> girls, weighing 7 lbs 15 oz. (3 kg 600 gm) between
> them. They are the most minute scraps I have ever

seen. It is a miracle that they are alive. They came to
us through one of our married girls and her husband. The latter, on hearing that we were willing to
take them, went off post haste, a few hours' journey,
and returned with three Nepali women, one the
grandmother, each bearing a very small bundle.
Kamla is in her element, giving herself day and
night, with extra help, in loving care.

Sadly, in September 1974, Muriel had to write that they
had had a nasty influenza epidemic in July and the
youngest triplet had died. Her little heart, never very
strong, could not stand the added strain. 'She had,'
Muriel wrote, 'just had her first birthday and she and
her bigger sisters in smart new garments and hair rib-
bons produced by Kamla were brought to greet us. The
youngest was such a merry little person, we are sure
she enjoyed her year with us, as we did to have her.
Kamla felt it deeply, but very soon a new tiny one of six
months came who needed much attention and shortly
after that a little two-day-old boy, so again her hands
are full.' Sadly one of the other triplets also died.

Writing in 1979:

Our office is part of the compound and before set-
tling to work, sounds of hearty singing came along
the path. Asha, the only surviving triplet, and a
character, with Romila, noted for cheerful disobedi-
ence and the pulling out of her hair, came into view,
arms round each other's necks and singing in Hindi
'Hallelujah, I am free, yes, I'm free from the burden
of my sin'. We hope it is prophetic! Anyway, the
work goes all the better for that interlude.

Muriel, even when most severe, never really lost the
twinkle in her eye! She was so pleased when her friend
Jean Cooke's GCU class in Oxford adopted Asha. They

were delighted that she grew up to marry, in 1996, a keen Christian man.

Kamla was sent away in the 1950s for special training at Bareilly in North India, and took over the supervision in Bethany (now called Bethlehem) of the small babies in 1954. She loved them all, the smaller the better, and pulled through many malnourished and premature babies, with day and night care and no special equipment. Muriel writing in 1981 in that same letter said, 'As Kamla, never lost for words, gave her testimony, I thought of a slide I showed in England in the 30s, Kamla with two others sitting under a tree in the Gorakhpur compound, entitled "the three little rebels". They were indeed. What a time we had with them. Now here is this capable woman, cheerful, loving, with an outstanding gift in the care of babies.'

Sadly Kamla developed diabetes in her forties and later, high blood pressure. One of her babies, Vidya, now grown up, felt called to help her. This was a wonderful preparation, for on 6th August, 1994, Kamla did not feel very well. Every month the Buas go to the bazaar for their big shopping day but this day Kamla elected not to join them. That evening she had a heart attack! She had never had one before, and she died within a few minutes. So her work and her 'family' were taken over by Vidya. Kamla was sixty-one.

Dr Rose Page, writing of Vidya in 1997 said

She is now 37. She came as a baby of three weeks and needing Kamla's special care. In school she was quite good at Maths, but could not retain facts in her memory and because of this failed exams. She did the 7th class twice, failed again and had to come out of school at the age of thirteen. As a result, she had a chip on her shoulder – most of her contemporaries went away to boarding school, some of them going on to Matric (10th), Intermediate (12th class) and then teacher training – and she had never even been away.

I am not sure at what stage she began to feel a definite call to stay on here, i.e. not get married, but stay especially to help look after the babies. No training was open to her, with her lack of schooling, but we were able to fix up four months' practical work in Raxaul, in midwifery and the Female and Children's Wards. This gave her status in the family and on her return she settled into Bethlehem and began to take on more responsibility from Kamla.

Over the next several years, all Vidya's age group departed, one by one, to marry and have their own homes. Then others, younger than Vidya, got married and she had no friends here of her own age. But she knew the Lord had called her to stay and as far as I know she never wavered.

Then on 6th August, 1994, Kamla died quite suddenly and unexpectedly, of a heart attack. Vidya was shattered – as indeed we all were – but soon rallied. She already had three children in her little family, but she immediately took on four more, varying in age from 7 to 21, so that they could all stay together in Bethlehem. She moved into Kamla's room and has become a real 'mother' there to this group, as well as to the babies. About three weeks after Kamla's death she was leading our senior Prayer Meeting and suddenly said, 'For years I have known that the Lord has called me to stay here, but only now do I see why'.

Today, Vidya not only looks after the babies and her own family but takes her turn at leading Prayer Meetings and the Sunday Services. She has a special gift for involving the children in songs (and even dance!). She has taken on from her bua Sharola, who died of cancer only ten days after Kamla, so Vidya was doubly bereaved in August 1994. Vidya has also taken on the tiresome job of getting rail reservations and sometimes when there are no tiny babies here, she acts as escort to our school girls on the overnight train to and from boarding school. She is becoming one of our spiritual leaders.

Another Bua was Chandraima. She came to the Nurseries, from Calcutta, when she was about eight years old, towards the end of the Second World War. She had been a 'mascot' in a British Regiment. They had given her a Khaki uniform to wear and she had wanted to go on wearing it when she came to Gorakhpur. She trained in 1955 to be a kindergarten teacher. She had quite a big family to look after and was wonderful at keeping in touch with those who had left to be married.

The Buas had to escort girls to and from school. This was work that Chandraima enjoyed and was especially good at. In 1995, she was bringing back a party of girls from school in Jhansi. Only ten to fifteen minutes after leaving Jhansi she had a stroke. There were seven senior girls with her who had just finished their O and A level exams (three O's and four A's). Several men in the carriage were helpful, they got ice when they stopped at the next station, as it was very hot, and the girls fanned her and tried to bring her round. But fourteen hours later when they reached Gorakhpur, she was still unconscious.

The Nurseries minibus had come to meet them and the driver managed to back it almost on to the platform and they got her into it. She never recovered consciousness, and died that day, about twelve hours later. She was fifty-nine. It was an awful experience for the girls, but with the Hindu attitude to death, and not touching dead bodies etc., it was a mercy she did not die on the journey.

This brings home, I think, how much more difficult it is to cope with all emergencies in a country like India than in most western countries.

Sharola was another very wonderful Bua. She came to the Nurseries as a baby from a village in Gorakhpur district. In about 1954, she went for junior teacher's training and qualified as a primary teacher. She taught for several years in Jainagar, where Muriel was of course in charge. When more younger teachers emerged, Sharola transferred to the outside work in dispensaries and villages. For most of her working life this was her main job becoming, in 1972, the leader of the dispensary team. She too looked after a large family of all ages.

The amount of work that they tackled in the dispensaries was really amazing. Writing in November 1978, Muriel said, 'The numbers in the Muktipur dispensary continue to increase and are up to 1,300 in a day, so that the team of six or sometimes five are hard pressed.' After discussing it with Sharola, who was in charge of the dispensaries, it was decided to move the one at Muktipur. There is the need always to keep 'open' and flexible even in seemingly 'established' work. The dispensary had been right on the main road, and so people just came in without real need, but after the move while the numbers continued high they were more manageable. None of the team were qualified as doctors or nurses, but God gave them amazing wisdom and skill as they looked to him to enable them to meet the tremendous need.

In 1981 Muriel wrote,

Sharola told of the work in the dispensaries, the patients for the year in two places [they were later to increase the dispensaries to three] Muktipur [Place of Salvation, five miles east of Gorakhpur] and Jainagar [Place of Victory – by the main road on their own compound] totalling 97,062, higher than any previous year. She spoke of individual cases of healing, of not always knowing how to prescribe but asking for guidance and then praying with the patient. She told of those who returned to give thanks and witness to the other patients. In Jainagar dispensary a man came for medicine for his wife with a serious goitre. He had been everywhere, tried everything, given offerings to idols to no avail. After two weeks of treatment, the woman was much improved and they decided to give up all idol worship.

Sharola is now in her forties [1981] and with the light in her face said 'It is the Lord's doing'. And it certainly is. The remedies used are tablets supplied by the Mission Tablet industry and simple home-made cough mixtures, ointments and powders. Sharola is tireless and selfless in this special bit of service.

Again, Muriel said, 'Watching her, we marvel and rejoice.'

Sharola had her finger in many pies. She was in charge of the Sunday School in the family, taking the top class herself every Sunday evening and ordering and looking after the books needed. She also often took evening prayers for the family and spoke at Sunday services.

She was very adept at getting reservations on trains, sometimes for more than sixteen school girls, which involved a personal visit to the Assistant Station Master. Anyone who has tried to make reservations on trains in India will know what a trying experience it can be.

Sadly, in May 1994, she was diagnosed as having cancer of the pancreas. She went to Ludhiana Christian Medical College where they felt surgery would not help but hoped that chemotherapy might. She had six weeks' treatment there and came home to continue her treatment, but she deteriorated quite quickly and died on 17th August, 1994. She was fifty-nine. The youngest of her children were distributed among the other Buas, while the older five or six stuck together as a little family.

One of the Buas mentioned in Muriel's day (in Chapter 18) was Pushpa. She is still with the family (1997) and Dr Rose Page, writing of her says,

Pushpa came to us from Ludhiana Hospital where she had been abandoned. Ludhiana was linked with The Nurseries, as Dr Brown, founder of the present Christian Medical College and Hospital, was friends with Aunt Molly and on the Fellowship Council. Pushpa was eight months old when she came. She was one of the seven in my very first class for daily Prayers when she was six or seven years old. I had only just begun learning Hindi. All I could do was say 'Sing' and they did – whether choruses or nursery rhymes I knew not. Then I'd point at one and say 'Pray'. For the lesson I would produce a picture, point to something in it and ask 'What is this?' Fortunately for Pushpa's Bible knowledge other people also were teaching her.

At school she did reasonably well, passing class 8, the highest class in our school (two years before matric). In those days, we only sent really bright people on to boarding school, education did not seem as important to a girl's future then as it is now. So Pushpa left school at fourteen and apart from six months at Kalvari Bible School, Allahabad, she has been helping at home ever since. She has never expressed any desire to marry and does not seem to mind that she is the only one of her age here (51 in 1997). For well over twenty years she has been our cook in Zion Cottage, the house in which Muriel lived. She says 'I love to serve'. Muriel worked with

her and taught her a lot of English cooking, jam-
making etc. Pushpa has picked up quite a lot of
English, working with us in the bungalow, and she
likes to try to speak English. She is not naturally a
motherly person but she does have a small family to
care for in Nazareth.

As there is a continuous need for girls to feel called to
stay on and work as Buas, so the need for husbands for
those who want to be married is continuous. The ever-
recurring subject of weddings, or lack of them, comes in
one letter. 'When filling in the register for 1988, I kept
coming to names of girls we had hoped to be married in
1987.' The girls have no way of finding husbands for
themselves, so they relied on Muriel and the others to
find them for them. This is, of course, in keeping with
the practice in India where arranged marriages are still
mostly the norm.

One of the girls called Light had hoped to get married, but at the last moment the proposed husband
postponed the wedding making all sorts of excuses.
When they finally realised he was not really sure the
wedding should go ahead it had to be cancelled.
Another feeler put out for her proved fruitless. A lot of
correspondence was needed for most arranged marriages. As Muriel said, 'Last year there were three weddings arranged by us but in the same period no less
than nineteen other parties were written to, inter-
viewed, photos sent, homes investigated, all with a neg-
ative result.' She said, however, how much better it is to
find out any snag before it is too late. Even with the
most careful investigations, some marriages do prove
disastrous. Recently one of the Tibetan nurses had to
flee with her two little children from her husband, a
Christian, but whose excessive drinking was making
him dangerously violent. They spent Christmas at the
Nurseries.

A lot of the marriages were encouraging, such as that of Ashalata who wrote and thanked Muriel and the others for their help. She lives in Kerala with her husband and two children. She wrote, 'How can I ever thank you. When I think how you brought me to the Saviour, Jesus Christ, I begin to cry with joy.' Another, who they describe as being such a naughty girl when she was with them, came back after twenty years of marriage with two keen Christian children. Some made their own arrangements, one that saddened them a lot was D. whose visit they had described as harrowing, as she had married a Moslem and was not happy.

The responsibilities and pressures of the family, even today, are always there.

20

TRANSPLANTATION

After she was refused Indian citizenship, Muriel, who had always imagined dying and being buried in Jainagar, began to wonder if God had other plans for her. This feeling was heightened by an increasing inability to walk due to arthritis, and more difficulty in enduring the hot weather. Elise Page and Ivy Hill had, in their latter days, always gone up to the hills during the hot weather. Sister Thilde and Muriel were finding they were also having to do so more than before. The Gordon sisters with whom they stayed in the hills were becoming increasingly frail and it was unlikely they would be able to go there much longer.

Muriel realised that, with increasing age (she and Thilde were both over eighty), they would become more and more dependent on the others and be a liability rather than an asset.

Elise Page and Ivy Hill had retired in 1972 to a cottage, St Aidans, in Blakeney. Elise died on 3rd February, 1979 and Ivy went on living in the house and then nearby, until she died on 8th October, 1980. It was a great surprise to Muriel and Sister Thilde to learn that she had left St Aidans to them.

Muriel, due to trying to get her Indian citizenship, had not been to England since 1961. So in 1981 she came home and went to Blakeney to see the house. She knew and loved it, having spent holidays in Blakeney, and Elise Page's sister Marian lived just up the road. She was a great friend of Muriel's.

There was a lot of clearing out needing to be done. Ivy Hill, on the never buy one if six will do principle, had all the store cupboards packed with tins, toilet rolls, paper towels, etc. What to do? Obviously the house could not be left empty; it was furnished and a lot of friends urged Muriel and Thilde to sell it. Muriel, however, in her spirit could not feel that was right. Before coming to England, she had put out feelers as to anyone who might be interested in taking on St Aidans as a holiday cottage. I had a friend Doreen (Jock) Haberman who I knew had links with Norfolk. She had just left as Principal of Romsey House, a Theological College in Cambridge and come to live in Heacham, Norfolk. She had handed over to Rev David Gregg and she wondered if he and his family might be glad of St Aidans as a bolthole from college life. This proved to be the case.

So before returning to India in 1981, Muriel drew up an agreement with Rev David Gregg for three years, which was later extended for a further three years. In her diary in 1987 she wrote,

I feel this is the End of an Era. Constant thought and prayer about what to do. Struck by the fact a number of things point to an ending, and leaving Gorakhpur. Praise the Lord. God's endings are always beginnings for Him.

Reasons for the feeling this is the right time to leave Gorakhpur:

1) The second three-year agreement with David Gregg for St Aidans ends in June 1987.
2) We will probably not be able to go and stay with Jo and Marj Gordon in the hills much longer. Marj herself had said 'I've been thinking about the future. I think we should just leave next year in the Lord's hand'. [Marj actually died in August 1987.]
[3] Arriving in Delhi in May 1987, Muriel felt she

couldn't cope with the journey again. So increasingly she was wondering if it was right for her to go and
occupy St Aidans herself. She said,] when one is
very old [she was eighty-three] everything becomes
too much, too many, too big, too quick, too heavy,
too long. I am ready now for the day of small things
and it is not to be despised (Zechariah 4:10). God has
eased the thought of going to England by giving me
St Aidans, and by having six weeks there six years
ago, so that I know and love the little place and can
think myself there before getting there. There will be
pain, not the pain of death and loss, but the pain of
birth and gain into something new. [Pretty good at
83? eh!]

So Muriel and Thilde, after much prayer and thought,
felt it was right for them both to leave Gorakhpur.

However no change goes unchallenged by the
enemy of souls, Satan. So Muriel wrote, 'Have had a
few days of Satan's taunting, you have mistaken the
guidance, and have made a horrible and irrevocable
mistake involving others etc. etc.' Then later she was
able to say, 'Today a wave of confidence and courage
flows in.'

Looking up in *Daily Light*, a small book of Scripture
portions for each day, the probable date of leaving
Gorakhpur, 28th March, 1988, she found these words:
'Be strong and be of a good courage. Arise therefore
and be doing and the Lord thy God will be with thee.'
She copied out the verse Jeremiah 29:11 in several translations.

For I know the plans I have for you, says the Lord,
plans for welfare and not for evil, to give you a
future and a hope. (RSV)

I keep in mind my purpose for you, a purpose of

weal not of woe, to let you have hope for the future.
(Moffatt)

I have not lost sight of My plan for you, the Lord
says, and it is your welfare I have in mind, not your
undoing; for you too I have a destiny and a hope.
(Knox)

For I know the thoughts and plans that I have for
you says the Lord, thoughts and plans for welfare
and peace and not for evil, to give you hope in your
final outcome. (Amp)

For I know the thoughts that I think toward you,
saith the Lord, thoughts of peace, and not of evil, to
give you an expected end. (AV. Margin said 'hope in
your latter end'.)

Thus she was comforted.

Thou will show me, mighty Father,
Step by step the wondrous way.
Side by side through time's long twilight
Press we to the drawing day.
Side by side we know not whither
But with whom we know full well.
Side by side, henceforth for ever
With Thee, veiled Emmanuel.
                              Author unknown

Muriel prayed and discussed it all with Thilde. She had
hoped that Thilde, who had been left St Aidans jointly
with her would come there and live with her. Thilde,
however, who in many ways would have loved to, felt
she should go back to Friedenshort, the Sisterhood in
Germany to which she belonged. It would not be easy
for her to slot back into a German-speaking community

after speaking mainly only English and Hindi over fifty years, but she knew that it was right to do so. Muriel had a great influence on her, but when Thilde felt something strongly, she put her foot down firmly and that was the end of the matter. It was so in the case of where she should retire.

Muriel, as she thought of the future, wondered what her ministry could be at home. In her diary she quotes William Barclay as saying that a retired Salvation Army officer in London in the blitz got together a surplus first aid box and put a notice in her window: 'If you need help knock here.'

Muriel wrote, 'I shan't put a notice in St Aidans but hope and pray it may become like that.'

Two of her favourite passages from the Psalms were,

Blessed is the man that walketh not in the counsel of the ungodly, nor standeth in the way of sinners, nor sitteth in the seat of the scornful. But his delight is in the law of the Lord; and in his law doth he meditate day and night. And he shall be like a tree planted by the rivers of water, that bringeth forth his fruit in his season; his leaf also shall not wither, and whatsoever he doeth shall prosper.

(Psalm 1:1–3)

The righteous shall flourish like the palm tree, he shall grow like a cedar in Lebanon. Those that be planted in the house of the Lord shall flourish in the courts of our God. They shall bring forth fruit in old age; they shall be fat and flourishing.

(Psalm 92:12–14)

Muriel wrote, 'To be a green leaf, a listening one – to have fruit in old age, that is my desire.' She wrote 'To give you an afterward. His plan – there will be a ministry. The Lord is speaking to me about the afterward.'

She'd had a letter requesting prayer for someone who had ankle ulcers – and for her daughter and two children, deserted by her husband. God said to Muriel, 'You will have a ministry by letter writing [which she certainly did] and by prayer [also true]. Your gift is to get alongside people (not meetings). I will be alongside, to enable and empower' (and he certainly did).

Mary Warburton Booth used to say to Muriel that she had the gift for writing, but she never felt inspired to write a book which is a pity because she could have written this book! She wondered how her gift was to be used. Someone had said of her, 'She doesn't make you feel shut out'. She wrote, 'I'm not interested in being just a friendly person, I want him to be in contact of my contacts and make them count for something.' God did this for her.

A good friend, when she heard I was writing a book about Muriel, wrote:

Here are my reminiscences of her – I have so many which must be like those of others. Very precious were the times one had alone with Muriel. From the time I first met her in the 1950s and 1960s I found it so easy to confide in her completely the most personal problems, knowing she would keep the confidence, but pray. This feeling continued when I visited Gorakhpur and especially in my visits to Blakeney which, after she returned, were about once a year. At the end of the day when we talked, read and prayed together, the fellowship was very sweet. Not just her prayers for my life, witness and problems but her breadth of concern for the whole world and this country, were a constant source of amazement to me. She was up to date with every wind of change in the Christian world and prayed with great insight and understanding.

So she and Thilde began to make definite plans to go home.

At the AGM in 1987, Muriel handed over the leadership of the Fellowship, a post she had held since Elise Page's retirement in 1972, to Dr Rosemary Page. Rose also became Secretary. Muriel had been Secretary of the Fellowship since 1948. Thilde handed over the treasurership of the Fellowship to Irene Rudling.

Then came the packing up, the goodbyes, none of which was easy after sixty years. Denise Earthy came out to India and then travelled home with them. They went first to the Deaconess House in Friedenshort, Germany, to which Sister Thilde belonged and where she was to stay. Then Denise and Muriel came on to St Aidans, Blakeney, which Denise had prepared for her arrival.

Still a member of the Gorakhpur Family, Muriel arrived back in England in March 1988, exactly sixty years since she had left for Gorakhpur, in March 1928.

21

RETIREMENT AT BLAKENEY

Blakeney, where Muriel came home to live, is a very charming old fishing village on the north Norfolk coast. This windswept area of sea, sand and salt marsh was once described, according to one of the books about Blakeney, as the best health resort in the kingdom. It certainly attracts many holidaymakers in the summer. There is National Trust parking down on the quay and, according to the tide, boat trips out to the Point to see the seals.

Muriel loved to go down to the quay, which was at the end of Back Lane where she lived. When she could walk she would go and sit and watch the sea, the birds, the people, quite contented for hours. Later when walking became more difficult she loved to be taken there.

It was good that Muriel was able to come back to a place that she had loved since a child. In a way its remoteness suited her very well. Holt, the nearest market town, five miles away, could only be reached by car, as could the nearest station, Sheringham, ten miles along the coast. There were no buses. There were, however, local shops within walking distance.

Soon after she got home in April 1988, she wrote in her diary, 'Again and again Jesus says "I am with you, I have made, I will bear".'

She of course kept in touch with the Nurseries and they with her, by letter. As I have said, she was a good letter writer and when she got down to it, enjoyed it. Although they now have a telephone at the Nurseries, they did not when Muriel was in Norfolk. Anyway, Muriel did not like the phone and avoided it if at all possible. She said she could not think clearly on it! Also, in her day, you did not spend money, except in dire emergencies, on long-distance phone calls.

After sixty years of living in a community, at the age of eighty-four to come home to live alone in England, having only been there for six weeks in the last twenty years, was quite an adjustment to make!

But with the serenity, humour and determination that had marked all her life, Muriel set out to tackle her new lifestyle.

One thing had not changed and that was her devotion to her Lord and her daily set aside Quiet Time and twenty-four-hour communion with him.

She wrote on 1st May, 1988,

> Vaguely thinking of expenses, He said out of the blue 'Trust in the Lord and do good, so shalt thou dwell in the land and verily thou shalt be fed – feed securely – feed on faithfulness.' Daily Light for that day: 'My people shall dwell in a peaceable habitation and in sure dwellings and in quiet resting places. Whoso hearkeneth unto Me shall dwell safely and shall be quiet from the fear of evil.' He also said, 'I would have you without carefulness '!

Always, however, with her feet on the ground, she wrote, 'This past week He has given two tokens for good. Heard through Sophie of someone to help in the house. Heard through Margaret of a possible man for the garden.' Later she wrote: 'My greatest need met, Angela Smith coming to help in the house. Had to wait but now have a gardener too.'

Blakeney has three church groups. Just up the road from St Aidans is St Nicholas Church, where Muriel's friend Marion Page went. The Rector, Nicholas Martin,

was very welcoming to her. So were the Methodists and
Judith Stephens in the next street. At the top of Back
Lane, just up the road from St Aidans, is St Peter's
Roman Catholic Church, built out of a converted
garage. Coming from an ecumenical background,
Muriel was soon friendly with all three leaders of the
churches. She found that the less rigid structure of the
Methodist Church really suited her best, but she also
went to the Parish Church and to a meeting called
Focalare.

She however recalled a meeting and talk at Focalare
where tolerance and love were the theme. She spoke of
feeling grieved in spirit, as there was no mention of
Jesus or reference to the Bible. Then the leader asked
Muriel to comment out of her wide experience. She
said, among other things, 'that we [the Gorakhpur fam-
ily] were accustomed to think in terms of black and
white, a more "faith and life" than "religion and
church" – and the Word says "Jesus is the only way to
God. Jesus only is the revelation of God and the way to
know Him" '. Then the leader turned to a man sitting in
the corner and said 'My beloved brother Asaf is a
Moslem.' Muriel recalls feeling awful, even though
three people came up to her afterwards and thanked
her for what she said. 'I am so glad you said what you
did, it needed saying.' 'You were absolutely right in
what you said.' But she remarked, 'I felt exhausted and
discouraged' and said she couldn't come again. She had
not realised that Focalare was an interfaith meeting.

Having spent most of her life bringing people out of
darkness into light, it hurt her to find westerners not
recognising darkness and by their attitudes condemn-
ing people to stay in it. She felt it was insulting to Jesus
and not really loving them, not to want them to come to
know Jesus, who alone said 'I am the light of the world'
(John 8:12; 3:19). The blurring of the Truth saddened
her. Muriel was having to find her way in the pluralis-

tic society England has become during the years she was away.

She made the comment, 'I keep hearing about born again Christians as if they belong to a sect, puzzling, as I have heard nothing good so far.' To Muriel, if you were a Christian, you were born again and you knew it. It was not a special odd brand of Christians! As she said, 'puzzling'.

The day after the Focalare meeting she went to a Lydia meeting. Lydia is an international fellowship, founded in 1970 by Shelagh McAlpine, wife of Campbell. Its stated aims are to 'alert, instruct and mobilise Christian women to pray, with fasting one day in each calendar month, with a prayer partner or in a small prayer cell, for the Church, Community, Country and nations of the world'.

Muriel really appreciated the Lydia Fellowship in England, though she surprised us all one day by saying she never fasted. It was just the sort of thing one imagined she would do! At her first Lydia meeting, they meditated on Hebrews 10:19 onwards. God spoke to her in verse 36: 'Don't draw back', verse 22: 'Draw near' and verse 23: 'Hold fast'.

She wrote, 'I believe I should continue to go to these gatherings and discussions, though I feel I would rather withdraw and be a hermit.' Later, the Lord told her to 'Put on the armour' (Ephesians 6:10–19).

When she was asked to speak at a Women's World Day of Prayer meeting, she writes of 'being horrified at being asked, but willing to do it if it really is the Lord's will'. She did it and was an excellent speaker. She felt, however, that her ministry was to be personal, to be on hand to help, rather than take meetings.

She recounts praying for a Blakeney lady, then meeting her in the Post Office and later in the day she arrived on the doorstep. To another, she really became a Spiritual Director. Muriel found it puzzling, the need for such terms as counsellor, Spiritual Director etc. To her, it all flowed naturally out of a life going on in the Lord.

She was asked to a house for drinks after church one Sunday and, feeling terrified, but being assured that the Lord was in control, she went. Someone at the drinks party (Muriel herself only drank soft drinks) said to her, 'I have seen you in the village, you have a friendly face'.

Most days she went up the road to see Marion, Elise Page's sister. She also planned trips further afield to see her old school friend, Dorothy Frears, who lived near Leicester.

She always enjoyed cooking and when they got the new Aga in the cottage, such remarks appeared in the diary as 'a domestic morning, washing, made a hot pot with a neck of mutton – delicious. Roast pork for lunch, again delicious. Kipper for supper, made sandwich cake, long call from Dorothy, got back, long call from Sylvia! Frantic! But it seems to have turned out all right. However, made flapjack and forgot it while talking, badly over cooked!' A friend wrote to say what a good cook Muriel was. This friend always tried to visit her when they could pick their own fruit for jam making something Muriel greatly enjoyed. The friend wrote: 'She was so excited about this and loved to come home and prepare to jam at once. Raspberries were her special delight and she was very expert at jamming them.'

Friends came to visit and she comments on their outings to Felbrigg Hall, Blickling Hall, the wonder of the sea coast between Blakeney and Cromer, the fields filled with daffodils, poppies, etc.

A great spirit of thankfulness invaded her whole life. She appreciated the fact that 'All good gifts around us are sent from heaven above', and she added her 'O thank the Lord, thank the Lord, for all His love'.

She was often very apt in her descriptions, as once after a shopping expedition she went into the Kings

Head for lunch. 'I was tired,' she said, 'and must have sat down heavily. A large elderly woman at the next table said to me, in a broad Norfolk accent, "That feel better don't it?" Had Norfolk hot pot and veg £2.40 each, served by enormous girl with bright yellow hair, clothed in tight puce pink dress.' Another time when a friend decided to arrive much later than expected, she comments, 'I'm rather on the jiffle'.

Commenting on a vicar and his wife, friends of a friend who visited, she said, 'I didn't take to them, she very much the Vicar's wife – good organiser – he, not very warm or outgoing.'

Someone at a meeting once asked her what she taught. She laughed and apparently replied, 'How to live'. To which the lady at once said, 'Come and tell me how to live'. Her comment on going to a church: 'Very few people in church and very dull.' Another service 'was lovely'.

Sidney and Dorothy Sims, a retired vicar and his wife from Cambridge called. They were living just round the corner. They became a very real help and support to Muriel. Dorothy took her to Women Aglow meetings, which she found really helpful.

She had always worn a sari in India and it being the easiest garment to wear she continued to do so on her return to England. However, during the winter months she surprised most of her friends by going into trousers, blouses and jumpers. She appeared very much at ease in them.

Muriel was tackling well every new challenge (there were many) that came along. She didn't, however, really enjoy living on her own. At one point in her diary she wrote, after being out, 'Glad to be back in warm house, leisurely tea with singing tapes – feeling extra isolated.' This isolation was relieved when Denise Earthy, a friend for some twenty-five years, decided to take early retirement and make St Aidans her home, a wonderful answer to prayer. When Denise was teaching in Wynberg Allen School in Mussoorie she often spent part of her holidays in Gorakhpur, and she had been a frequent visitor at St Aidans after Muriel came. (She it was who went out to travel home with Muriel and Thilde when they left Gorakhpur in 1988.) Another great joy for Muriel was that Thilde was able to come to visit; Denise would go over and fetch her and take her back.

So her days of 'small things' began and they were certainly not to be despised.

Friends like Dorothy Frears and many others who had visited her in her last years in India were delighted to have her home and to be able to ring and see her. On one of her visits to Dorothy, Muriel wrote: 'Like most aged people, we reminisce, compare notes on our reactions and put the world to rights.'

Sadly Norah Lloyd, one of her three original school friends, had died just before Muriel got home. That was a great loss to Muriel as she had looked forward to seeing and talking with her. Norah had been such a faithful friend all those years in India, sending out and organising the newsletters etc. The third friend of her school days, Phyl Stanley, had died several years before. So only Dorothy was left.

Muriel was also pleased that Paddy (Jean) Cooke could visit. She was a great friend of Norah's and had visited Muriel in Gorakhpur. On one visit Muriel wrote, 'Paddy suggested a run in the car. Went to Moreston Marshes – glorious sunset – couldn't leave. Got home 10.15 p.m.' That was late for Muriel, who always made a point of going to bed early – in Gorakhpur it had been 8.30 p.m. Mind you, she got up early, as she had in Gorakhpur, when she could be found on the job at 6 a.m.

She was delighted to have Rose Page's brother, Rev Dick Page and his wife Sue, nearby in Norfolk. They often visited. One time when Thilde was over on her birthday, Muriel wrote, 'Dick, Sue and Charlotte (their daughter) 10.30 for coffee then 11.30 picnic lunch (super, thanks to Denise) at Blickling Hall. We went round gardens, Sue produced wheelchair for Thilde. We had lunch in orchard at a picnic table. Then we looked round National Trust shop – had tea in their tea room – scones, jam and cream! Back by 6 p.m. lovely day – couldn't have been better!'

So with Denise there most of the year, local people welcoming her into the life of the community and many friends, new and old who were supporters of the work in Gorakhpur visiting her, Muriel passed her first year at home in Blakeney.

By 1991, she was beginning to find everything too much. She wrote to me, 'You might pray the Lord will control our visitors. I find it rather much when it is incessant and unexpected.' It was however an indication of her popularity. She found herself increasingly unable to cope with standing for a long time to cook etc. and was feeling that she would become a burden to Denise, which she did not wish to be. So she started putting out feelers as to where she might go. She had always known of Rosset Holt in Tunbridge Wells, as a retirement home for missionaries. An old friend, Evelyn Giles, had been chairman and was still on the committee. Evelyn was delighted at the prospect of Muriel coming and wrote and said, 'This place was made for you'. It was founded with the idea of being especially for missionaries who had served many years overseas and had no home in England, to come and retire to.

However suitable she was for Rosset Holt and they for her, she still very sensibly had to go according to the rules and have a trial week there to see if she really felt it right.

There were several hitches before she could go, since they were decorating the hall, stairs and landings.

However eventually she went in February 1992 and all were in agreement that it was the place for her although there was only a small room vacant at that time.

She wrote in March:

> I am getting forward with things that need seeing to and things I need for going to Rosset Holt, so that when Thilde comes we can enjoy the time. It is lovely that we can have a last time together at Blakeney. I have written to Evelyn to tell her that I could come mid-August. I think they have their committee meeting next week, so I hope to hear something definite, especially about the room. I have made a plan to scale and can see how the furniture will fit in – the great thing will be to keep it uncluttered and yet have enough for when and if I move into something larger.

In the event, she did go in August 1992 and into a lovely big downstairs room with a bay window with a wide sill, on which she could put all the plants and flowers she loved so much.

I was pleased, as the cottage in Matfield which I was left when I came home from Nepal, was only five miles from Tunbridge Wells. Also lovely for both of us was that I was given a car, and passed my driving test just a week before she came to Rosset Holt.

When I visited her in her lovely sunny room, I used to tease her and say, 'You know two people had to die so you could have this room.' It was actually true that the two previous occupants had died during the time Muriel was waiting to come!

The Nurseries, as we know, never appealed for funds. In Blakeney, the cost of living was much higher than it had been in Gorakhpur. Muriel had no pension but had a little capital, left to her by her father. She managed, with gifts from friends, to live on this.

However, the costs at Rosset Holt were going to be more than she could manage. She insisted on paying the first month, then very wonderfully, a Fund linked with the Gorakhpur Nurseries, called the L.F. Fund, was available to pay for her, proving that 'those who trust him wholly, find him wholly true' and 'seek first the Kingdom of God and his righteousness and all things will be added to you'. Once again, her needs were met.

So began a new chapter in Muriel's life.

22

ROSSET HOLT

When Muriel arrived at Rosset Holt in August, the room looked lovely. She brought with her bulbs and pot plants and these she quickly arranged on the big sill of the bay window. She put her large armchair by the window and had a lovely view over the lawn, flower beds and trees of the very pretty garden. Muriel was essentially a homemaker and she set about, as soon as she arrived, to make her room her home. The pieces of furniture and other belongings that she had brought from Blakeney fitted in remarkably well. Her bed behind the door had a lovely blue patchwork quilt from India on it. On the wall was a picture of the family in Gorakhpur and behind her bed the wooden plaque I mentioned at the beginning, with the words: 'Make the omnipotence of God the measure of your expectation'.

She managed very successfully to stamp her personality on the room and it gave you a sense of warm welcome and a Presence as soon as you entered it. Also that 'uncluttered' feel that she had so wanted. There were two chairs for visitors placed so you could easily sit and chat with her while being able to enjoy the garden too. They were conveniently put by a table on which was a kettle to make a cup of tea or coffee. Given to hospitality, she carried on now, with very restricted facilities, the traditional welcome she had always given to visitors she knew and loved, and she had many now, friends in the south who hadn't been able to see her before came and others, when they discovered where she lived,

turned up too. Both old and new friends enjoyed a
wonderful sense of fellowship when they visited.
Muriel retained such a deep personal interest in each
one and in their affairs and Christian ministry.

The toilet and telephone were conveniently placed
off a utility room nearby; she could reach these easily
with the help of the stick she now used. There was a
curtained-off wash basin in her room. Meals were
served in the large front hall with eighteen residents
round the two polished tables. The staff also ate at the
same time, serving the meals and sitting at a separate
table. The food was good, though I often thought they
could have benefited from some hints from Muriel and
I know in her heart of hearts she felt the same.

She knew some of the other residents as many too
had been in India and other places as missionaries; one
had been the Principal of a Bible College. But not all had
been missionaries. Long-term missionaries now becoming a dying breed, the home had been changed to be a
home for Christian ladies.

Muriel did not have difficulty in finding which
church to go to. Friends from India, Ted and Joy
Lankester went to St Mark's, Broadwater Down,
Tunbridge Wells. It was her sort of church, a charismatic-
type service, with a lot of reverent worship and quiet
periods too. St Mark's also has a more traditional service later in the morning, but Muriel always went to the
earlier non-traditional one! She took at once to the vicar,
Rev Francis Cumberlege and his wife Tina. Francis
often visited her, and said at her Thanksgiving Service
what a blessing it was to him to do so.

She appreciated the services in the house,
Communion taken by Rev Norman Norgate, Vicar of St
James nearby, as well as the fellowship and prayer
meetings. She enjoyed going to a Monday morning
Lydia group in the area. She went as often as she could.

Joy Devis (who I mentioned in Chapter 17), now she

was near, was a frequent visitor and took Muriel to stay with her. She probably had more regular trips out than anyone else in the home. She loved to go to the sea and was quite happy, in fact liked to be left in my car, parked on the front, near the loos at Bexhill, to just snooze, or look at the sea and passers-by while I went to visit friends there.

The Bible says 'godliness with contentment is great gain' (1 Timothy 6:6). Muriel proved this is so. She did not like to be idle and when she heard of the need for knitted cot covers and other blankets in Romania, she set about knitting squares and got practically everyone else in the house doing so too. Often when I was visiting her, different ones would come in with squares they had done. It, of course, gave them an interest too. The squares had to be joined up and a lot of this she did herself. There are, however, notes in her diary such as Tuesday 29th: 'Assembled two cot covers with Mary Jane, Dulcie and Dora now on team of joiners, great help.' She loved going to garden centres to buy bulbs, plants etc. for the window sill which she always kept beautifully. There are notes she made such as, 'Got seeds calendula, lobelia and geranium, sowed them and re-arranged pots and turned out cyclamen.'

She was glad in 1993 when Kathleen Robertson, who had been in India, came. They were able to do a lot of things together. Kathleen had local contacts, having come from nearby Wadhurst.

In April 1994, aged 90, Muriel fulfilled a desire she had had for many years – to go to a big residential Christian event in England. She, Kathleen, Rose Page home from Gorakhpur, and Denise Earthy went to Spring Harvest at Skegness, combined ages 306. She was thrilled with it. She wrote, 'Wonderful accommodation suites, Kathleen 3 rooms 4 beds, me 3 rooms 5 beds, Denise and Rose 3 rooms 4 beds, all with bath and loo, very comfortable, heated, TV, electric jug and nothing extra to pay! Went to evening meal, roast lamb ++, apple pie and cream. Then to meeting at 7 – lovely worship, came away 9.30 – deadly tired, dropped into bed without doing anything!' So she goes on recording everything with great zest. 'Decided to go once to meeting in Big Top.'

As they arrived, pushing Muriel in her wheelchair, the sidesman said, 'Come on girls'. Muriel's comments are, 'Very noisy, discordant. Peter Meadows, London Radio, spoke – very good, came away after he had spoken.' However she went to quite a few of the meetings and enjoyed them. Rosemary got an awful cold and cough and Denise slipped and sprained her ankle, so that on the last morning Kathleen and Muriel went to breakfast on their own. Muriel's comment in her diary 'Well done oldies!' When she got home, she wrote, 'Slept like a log!'

She maintained her evangelistic zeal to the end, and was very enthusiastic about a new outreach on a nearby housing estate. She prayed regularly and with knowledge as she would go as often as she could to the meetings there.

It being difficult for Thilde to come over to England, Denise took Muriel to Friedenshort, which was, of course, a great joy.

Muriel was a great lover of animals and she missed not having a pet. She speaks of someone bringing in three puppies and they being lovely to cuddle but 'weep-making'! So she and Kathleen felt they would like to have a pet or pets. After talk and thought they decided two guinea pigs would be a good idea. They asked Matron and she said that it would have to be a committee decision. The committee decided that they could have them 'six months on probation'. As Muriel's room was on the ground floor and had a side door it was not too difficult for them to be kept in a cage there. There were then great expeditions to buy the guinea pigs, get the cage etc. They called them Tiggy and Honey. They brought a lot of pleasure to them, coming into Muriel's room to be loved!

Muriel kept remarkably well. She did have to have one spell in Maidstone Hospital when she fell and broke her femur. For her age she made a remarkably quick recovery. I was amazed how good she was in hospital, as I knew she hated them and anything to do with illness. I was surprised when one day, late in 1994, she said to me 'I do hope I never have to go into hospital again; it was awful, I really dread it.' So I, on the spur of the moment said, 'Well, let's pray that you never will have to.' So we both stopped and made it a matter of prayer, 'If two of you shall agree as touching anything, it shall be done' (Matthew 18:19). And left it at that. In February 1995, I went off to visit Nepal and Muriel was in very good health, so much so that I joked, 'Now don't go and die while I'm away, will you?'

On April 1st I had a phone call in Kathmandu, Nepal, to say Muriel had died the day before, 31st March, 1995. She had gone to stay with Joy Devis and they had had a lovely time going out on Box Hill, walking together. On her second day with Joy, Muriel started complaining of indigestion-type pains and feeling sick. Joy, a nurse, rang the doctor, who couldn't come at that time. Muriel expressed a desire to go back to Rosset Holt and Joy decided, having rung Rosset Holt, to take her. The doctor there came to see her but later she suddenly felt sick again, sat up and died. Kathleen Robertson and Evelyn Giles were with her.

The funeral service was at Rosset Holt and then later, on Thursday, 22nd June, a Thanksgiving Service was held at St Mark's Church, Broadwater Down.

One of the speakers, Geoff Williams, had to get a taxi from Tunbridge Wells station to the church. As they were going along, the taxi driver asked him, 'Are you going to something good, sir?' 'Oh yes,' said Geoff, 'I'm going to a celebration.' It certainly felt like that. One of the Rosset Holt ladies said they had never been to anything like it before.

We sang one of her favourite hymns, which in a way summed up her life.

> I've found the Pearl of greatest price,
> My heart doth sing for joy,
> And sing I must, a Christ I have,
> Oh, what a Christ have I.

> My Christ He is the Lord of Lords,
> The Sovereign King of Kings,
> The risen Sun of Righteousness
> With healing in His wings.

> My Christ, my Father and My Friend
> My Brother and my Love,
> My Head, my Hope, my Counsellor,
> My Advocate above.

> My Christ He is my Heaven of heavens,
> My Christ what shall I call?
> My Christ is First, my Christ is Last,
> My Christ is All in all.

A few weeks later, about ten of us went out in a boat with Rev Nicholas Martin and Rev Judith Stephens, to Blakeney Point and scattered Muriel's ashes on the sea she loved so much. As Judith wrote to me afterwards, 'How Muriel would have enjoyed the boat trip, chuckled at every wave that soaked us to the skin and delighted at the huge sky, with its grey clouds yet air that was warm and mellow.'

Judith, who had only known Muriel in retirement, at the short service in the Methodist Church before the boat trip, summed up much of Muriel's life when she

said, 'Muriel joined us at the Methodist Church, but
equally she shared worship at St Nicholas. She was
truly ecumenical.' She went on,

Knowing that she had time in retirement (we all
assume that the retired have nothing to do!) I asked
her to be my Spiritual Director – a grand name for
the privilege of being the punch bag for all my emo-
tions, reactions, worries, joys and distress. She
agreed to be a listening ear, and she was, but she
was more than that . . . she heard the things I was
NOT saying and she asked searching questions until
the real needs surfaced. She offered her thoughts
(she would never presume to call it advice), she
would pray with me and for me, and her interest in
my life in all its aspects was total. Nothing was
unimportant or stupid – if it concerned me, it was
real and needed expression. Not that she agreed
with me all the time, far from it, she was my mentor
in the true sense of the word.

   She somewhat vainly insisted that I should have
regular 'play days' and forced the issue by inviting
me to go on picnics etc.

   She was horrified to know that, although I've lived
around here for fifty of my fifty-four years, I had
never been to Blakeney Point or indeed out to sea
(beyond waist deep when swimming). When I heard
of the idea of scattering her ashes out to sea, I wondered if she would yet get her wish. I'm not sure if it
was her idea or Denise's, but I can well imagine her
chuckling this morning as we board the boat.
Certainly her spirit will be with us as we move
across the water. I consider it a great privilege to be
there too.

   When Muriel moved to Tunbridge Wells, she
wrote regularly and still heard the unspoken word.
She was good at reading between the lines and to

the end of her life she was there for me, answering my questions, guiding my thinking. But not just for me, what she did for me, she did for others also, maybe in a different way, but caring was for all who crossed her path. She loved HUMANITY in general and those she knew in particular. We knew her for such a short time, but it was a blessed time. She was a rare jewel and precious to us all.

After Muriel died, I found the following among her papers, which again I feel is very typically 'Muriel'.

August 16th 1972 (when she was 69 and was taking over the leadership of the Nurseries) she wrote:

Be positive in thinking and talking. Mind and thoughts affect health.
Don't talk about getting old and not being able to do things.
Psalm 104:16 'The trees of the Lord are full of sap' (satisfied).
Psalm 92:10 'I shall be anointed with fresh oil', verses 12 – 14 'Those that be planted in the house of the Lord shall flourish in the courts of our God, they shall still bring forth fruit in old age; they shall be fat and flourishing' (full of sap and green).
Blossom where you are planted.

We are meant to be healthy, full of sap, satisfied,
        fresh oil, fat and flourishing, full of sap – green.
Because anointed and satisfied and dwelling in the courts of the Lord.
Because planted by Him. Fruitful right up to the end.

Joshua 1:2 'Moses my servant is dead' – past
        'Now you arise' – present
A linking by God of past, present and future –

'a continuance'

Moses didn't finish. Joshua didn't finish.

Both in their farewell addresses link past with present.

The Lord says to Joshua at the end of his life and service, Joshua 13:1: 'There remaineth yet very much ground to be possessed.'

The Lord said to Moses – Deuteronomy 32:52

'Thou shalt see the land before thee'

Moses should see what all his life and service had been leading to.

Even if he had gone in, his service, the work, would not have been finished

The Lord says –

Muriel my servant is dead. Now you arise and enter into your promised land.

Make the Omnipotence of God, as Muriel did, the measure of your expectation.

EPILOGUE

So the work of the Gorakhpur Nurseries Fellowship continues.

There are about eighty-six now in the present family and a few new babies and children who are abandoned or for one reason or another have no home are each year, as before, added to the family.

Rosemary Page is in charge with Irene Rudling helping her. Recently, in 1996, to everyone's great joy, they have been joined by an Indian colleague, Mrs Harriet Sankaradas. She comes with many years of experience of working in the Interserve Office in Delhi. She is a great asset, as among many other things she is able to work on the computer!

Agnes Gilruth, Frances Backhouse and Maryke all had to leave the work in Semri (God's Garden) which the Gorakhpur Nurseries started in Nepal. They were pleased to be able to hand it over to Indian Christian workers. The dispensary work has now been taken over by the Government but not before a church had been planted in the area.

If anyone is interested to know more about the work, you can write to:

Dr Rosemary Page at The Gorakhpur Nurseries Fellowship, Post Box 43, Gorakhpur, U.P. 273001, India.

It is possible to become a prayer partner and also to take an interest in a particular child. Regular news is sent of the girls to their prayer partners.

If you should be interested to know how God opened up his work in the land of Nepal, also how God used Muriel and Thilde to bless me, you can read it in my book *Better Than The Witchdoctor*, obtainable

from Christian Bookshops or Interserve, 352
Kennington Road, London, SE11 4QH.